CIVILIZATION

The Civilization of the American Indian

Thomas Wildcat Alford in Tribal Dress

CIVILIZATION

AND THE STORY OF THE ABSENTEE SHAWNEES

AS TOLD TO

FLORENCE DRAKE

BY

THOMAS WILDCAT ALFORD

WITH A FOREWORD BY ANGIE DEBO

UNIVERSITY OF OKLAHOMA PRESS : NORMAN

To Those Who
Admire Indian Character
This Book Is Dedicated

FOREWORD

IT is a pleasure to welcome Thomas Wildcat Alford's *Civilization* back to print. It relates the firsthand experiences of a Shawnee Indian born in 1860, who grew up in a remote portion of the Indian Territory not far from the present Shawnee, Oklahoma. It is a revealing human document, for the narrator knew only an Indian childhood, but through the educational policy of his time eventually became a white man in all but blood.

As it came to him through the roseate hues of happy memories he may have idealized somewhat the Indian society of his early years, but his descriptions of procedures and customs can be trusted—from his explanation of social and community institutions and living techniques to his mother's cooking recipes. But that area of the Indian Territory was losing its isolation. At the age of twelve the boy began attending a school started by the Quakers, and soon taken over by the United States Indian Service. He knew only one English word when he entered, but by the end of four years he had the rudiments of an English education.

Soon the head men of the tribe decided to send him and another young man to Hampton Institute for further study. These conservative leaders, wholly committed to the Indian way, felt the need of training some selected youths to circumvent the white man's tricks of learning. It did not work out as they had planned. After a 120-mile drive through an undeveloped wilderness to the nearest railroad station at the squalid little town built on Creek soil at Muskogee the two youths took the train for the East. A routine journey in the white man's book, it became a great adventure when seen through young Indian eyes—the unimagined splendor of cushioned seats and carpeted aisles, the views from the windows of bustling cities and a productive countryside—"A wonderland indeed!" as he remembered it, which seemed not only desirable but attainable.

At Hampton he found that the training had been planned to fit the Indian students not only with the necessary vocational skills, but even with the most trivial usages of white society. He became wholly committed to the new life way, and the opportunity of bringing these advantages back to his people was his sustaining faith during the three years of intensive study he spent at Hampton. (His companion remained somewhat longer and returned to become a successful merchant.)

But Alford, still loving his people and dedicated to helping them, experienced a heart-breaking rejection. He finally found work with the local Indian Service, first as a teacher, then at the agency; and this became his lifetime career. Not once did he question the official policy of merging the Indians into a composite American citizenship. He even approved the liquidation of tribes and tribal land holdings under the Dawes Act of 1887 and similar legislation, a policy stoutly resisted by the Indians of the Territory. Thus he worked conscientiously at "allotting" an individual farm to each fellow Shawnee and the members of neighboring tribes, explaining the advantages of this system of ownership; and he watched with interest as the "surplus," left over from the allotments, became available for white settlement, thus becoming a part of the process that transformed the Indian Territory into the lusty, striving frontier that was Oklahoma.

Then the inevitable happened, a criminal conspiracy to cheat the Indians out of their allotments. So far as it related to the Shawnees and their neighbors it involved local grafters centered in the new, growing city of Shawnee and their confederates among high government officials at Washington. The plot consisted of gaining the confidence of the Indians and persuading them to abandon their allotments— to be acquired by the conspirators—and remove to an imaginary paradise in Old Mexico, where they could continue their native ways. The Indian Service fought the scheme, which would have reduced the Indians to homeless wanderers. Much of the work fell on the local agency; and Alford, who still retained contact with his people, served actively in defending them. The fight dragged on for years in administrative and legislative action and through the courts, and the Indians' case was finally won—after a fashion. Alford regarded his own contribution to the victory as "one of the proudest achievements of my life."

He did not name the prominent Washington officials who used their political influence to further the conspiracy, but he planned "to file a true account" with the Oklahoma Historical Society "because it rightly belongs to the history of the Oklahoma Indians." Truly it does. Years later, Arrell M. Gibson through intensive research ferretted out and published the whole plot as it was directed against the neighboring Kickapoos; but in general, Oklahoma historians have avoided all mention of the wholesale plundering of Indians that followed the division of their tribally owned land. Apparently even Alford failed to file his "true account" for future reference, for it has not been found in any known depository. And although he condemned the swindlers, he still supported the policy that gave them the opportunity for plunder. The white man's way was still the better one. And no doubt it was, for him. A letter written at the time by one of his young sons is eloquent of the wholesome, happy life the family lived, socially and at home on the farm.

He ends his book by predicting that the Indians would eventually lose their identity as a race, but that their influence would remain as a permanent contribution to "the sterling qualities of the American character." This goal—at least as imposed forcibly—is now out of favor, but the reading of Alford's story affords a new and fresh experience of familiar developments in our history as felt from the inside looking out.

Angie Debo

May 1, 1979

PREFACE

THE pleasure of preparing this manuscript for publication has been marred only by my inability to convey the ideas presented by Mr. Alford in exactly his own words, thus losing much of their beauty and significance. However, the patience with which he has labored all the years of his life for his own people has been extended to me in this work, and I can only hope that the sympathetic understanding of the reader will give the interpretation which I have failed to convey.

FLORENCE DRAKE

Tecumseh, Oklahoma

CONTENTS

CIVILIZATION

Thomas Wildcat Alford At Work

ANCESTORS

I

I WAS born in 1860, according to my parents, "about the time blackberries were ripe," which probably would mean about July 15. I was the second child—I had a sister two years older than I. My parents with other members of their tribe, Absentee Shawnee Indians, had been given permission by the friendly Creeks, or Muskogee Indians, to settle in the Creek country, after the forcible removal of the Shawnees from their former reservation in the state of Texas. At the time I was born my parents were living on the bank of the Canadian River, near the site of the present town of Sasakwa, in Seminole County, Oklahoma.

My father, whose Indian name was Gay-tah-ki-piah-si-kah (meaning lying-spotted-in-the-brush, hence he was called Wildcat) was of mixed blood, having had an English captive for his grandmother. His father was Se-leet-ka, son of chief Kik-us-kaw-lo-wa, who signed three treaties with the United States government for the Shawnees.

The story of the capture of my father's English grandmother always has been an interesting one to me, although it does not reflect very creditably on the party of scouting Shawnee braves who took her from her family when she was a small child. The scouts brought the baby to the chief's wife, who was childless. She loved the little white girl very dearly, and cared for her as tenderly as she knew how to do. The child grew, and played happily with the Indian children.

[1]

When the little captive, who was called We-pay-que-lee-qua (gray eyes), was a girl of fourteen years the Indians entered into a treaty with the government whereby they were to give up all white captives, and the little English girl was restored to her own family. But she loved the Indians and their wild, free way of living, and pined for her foster mother so much that she was very unhappy when separated from her.

Finally the maiden made up her mind to return to the Indian village and her foster parents, and made her plans with all the cunning she had learned from the Indians. When her plans were mature she arranged for an absence from her own home, by going for an extended visit with some relatives. But no sooner had she reached the home of her relatives, and her own family thought she was safe, than she pretended that she must return to her own home. Her relatives, thinking nothing of her change of mind because they expected eccentricities in her conduct due to her long residence with the Indians, allowed her to set out alone for her own home. Instead of going home she started in the direction of the Indian country. Again she used the cunning she had learned from the Indians, and traveled as best she could, on foot, swimming streams, eating wild fruit and grain she could find in fields, dodging about, avoiding white settlements, until at last she reached an Indian village. There she was shielded, and finally helped to return to her foster parents.

In the meantime the girl's foster mother, the wife of the Indian chief, had grieved so deeply over the loss of her daughter that it was thought she would not live. She refused to eat food, and pined away. Finally she was no longer able to go about, but lay on her bed in an exhausted condition, seemingly waiting for life to leave her body, while her mourning friends watched beside her.

Then one day there was a great commotion in the Indian village. The people were stirred with excitement! We-pay-que-lee-qua had returned.

Those watching at the bedside of the sick woman noticed a change come over her, then she sat upright on her couch —the young girl approached, and they were clasped in each other's arms, happy to be reunited. The foster mother was no longer ill; she rapidly regained her strength, and lived to an old age. The little white girl was hidden from the prying eyes of anyone who might report her presence among the Indians. She grew into womanhood and became the wife of Kik-us-kaw-lo-wa, and the mother of eight sons, one of them being Se-leet-ka, my own grandfather.

My mother was called Way-lah-ske-se (one of grace) and never bore an English name. Her father was Nay-thah-way-nah, son of the celebrated Shawnee warrior Tecumseh.

When I was ten days old I was given a name, in accordance with the custom of our people, by an old friend of the family. Therefore I belonged to the same social clan or Um-so-ma[1] as the person who named me. The name given me was Gay-nwaw-piah-si-ka (one of long following or file, as the leader of a drove of wild horses) which soon was shortened to Gay-nwah, for the same reason that Thomas is shortened to Tom. No surname was used among the Shawnees.

Had I been a girl my parents would have waited two days longer before I should have received my name, which in all probability would have been the same (with the last

1. There are six branches of Um-so-ma (good genius is the nearest English expression to the Indian meaning of Um-so-ma), which is a kind of social clanship existing between members of the Shawnee tribe. When a child is named he automatically belongs to the same Um-so-ma as the person who named him. The comradeship and partisanship existing between members of the same Um-so-ma is outstanding, and the cause of merry rivalry and much innocent fun. It is not to be confused however with the tribal clan divisions which constitute the government of the tribe.

[3]

syllable left off to denote gender), if the same Um-so-ma had been desired to be represented in the name. A child always is classed in the same social clan with the person who names him, is considered under the same kind providence or care. This clan division is the occasion of strong partisanship and much pleasant rivalry among the Shawnees. It is simply a social division and should not be confused with the real clanship of the tribe, which determines the chieftainship and in fact the very existence of the tribal organization, and is fully explained in another chapter.

I never was told anything that would indicate that I was different from other little Indian babies. Boys usually were desired more in Indian families than were girls, and I suppose that as I was the first boy born to my parents they were proud of me and gave me a little more attention than usually was accorded a baby. I know that my parents were considered above the average in intelligence, and gave their children more care than many of our people gave to their children.

My mother carried me on her back, strapped securely to a board which was called a *tkith-o-way*, as did other Indian mothers of that time. This tkith-o-way was carved and ornamented according to the taste of the parents, even as a baby carriage of today is often indicative of the pride and prosperity of the parents.

Indian mothers carried their babies on their backs for several reasons. The first was for the safety of the child. Wild animals often invaded the settlements, and it would not have been safe to leave a young child unprotected in the crude cabins of those days. The mother's work often took her away from her home for hours, and she generally had some burden to carry, besides her child, as she went about her daily tasks. With the child securely strapped to its tkith-o-way, and that swung on her back, her arms were free for the work to be done, or to carry implements she might need for her work, a jug of water, or whatever burden she had to carry. Another reason for strapping the child to a tkith-o-way was to make the little back grow straight and strong. Then too, the little head was bound closely to the flat surface to make it grow flat, so that when he reached maturity there would be a flat spot on the back of his head where a plate would fit, to which could be attached an eagle feather, the desired headdress of a Shawnee brave.

My mother was typical of the Indian woman of that time: strong, vigorous, and self-reliant. Her patience and fortitude were unfailing, her courage undaunted and contagious. I believe too that she was intelligent, far beyond the average woman of her time. She took upon herself the burden of providing for her family, not only doing those housewifely tasks expected of the women of today, such as the preparation of food, the making of clothing for her children, and the general care of the home and family, but much more. In those days the Indian women planted and cultivated all crops. She plowed or dug the ground, planted the corn or other seed, cultivated it, then harvested it. She ground the corn into flour or meal with which she made bread for her family; she dressed the game that her husband brought home and tanned the hide—if it was fit to be used— and she cured the meat.

My mother did all these things during those early years of my recollection, but I can remember that father gradually took upon himself more and more of this labor, as the family increased, and he no doubt saw the injustice of leaving so much of the hardest work for a woman to do.

The years of my babyhood, 1860-1861, were years of great agitation among all the Indians of the Old Indian Territory, as well as among all the citizens of the nation. The Civil War had commenced between the Northern and the Southern states, which, as everyone knows, was caused by the questions of slavery of the Negro race, and states' rights. The people of the Southern states believed that each state had a right to enact its own laws (relative to the holding of slaves), and the Northern states insisted upon the abolition of slavery in all states. A great many of the Indians were in sympathy with the Southern states; others were loyal to the Union.

The events of those early years of my life are allied so closely with the history of our people and our country, and I have heard them told and retold so many times and discussed so much from every point of view, that I can hardly distinguish between my personal recollection and things I have heard my elders relate. But the facts are firmly established in my memory, and I shall, to the best of my ability, relate them here in their proper sequence.

The Absentee Shawnees were associated in their councils with several other tribes: the Tallihassee Town of Creeks, the Delawares, the Piankeshaws, and the Kickapoos. These all held councils together; their leaders said, "This is no fight of ours. It is between the whites—no good comes to us from war—let them fight their own fight," and their people all agreed to do that.

About that time Micco Hutke of Tallihassee Town and Robert Deer of the Shawnee tribe made a trip to Washington and visited President Lincoln. He told them the same thing.

"This is no fight of yours; it is between the white people. You keep out of it. If you cannot remain in your country in peace, come out of it, and if you lose property the government will pay you for it."

Satisfied with this promise they returned home.

But in spite of all the counsel they had received and their own determination to keep out, the Indians were gradually being drawn into the quarrel. They had friends on both sides and were being solicited continually to take part. Most of the Creeks were in sympathy with the new government in the South, but others were standing firm for the United States, with whom all their treaties were made. Our own people were bewildered and did not know which way to turn.

By 1862 the times actually were dangerous, because of so much dissension among the Indians. In that year came John Rogers and other Shawnees who lived in Kansas to visit us. They learned of the trouble our people were in and invited us to come to the Shawnee reservation in Kansas, since they were our brothers. Kansas had not entered into the war, and the Shawnees believed they were out of its range.

Our people did not want to leave their homes. They had crops growing; some had cattle and hogs. They did not accept the invitation at that time. But there was no way to keep out of the trouble where they were. Both sides of the controversy (among our friends) insisted that we take sides, that we express ourselves, show upon which side our sympathies lay. At that time it was a question of sympathy, more than of actual participation. It was almost impossible to remain neutral.

Finally a secret council was held in which several tribes took part—secret because they were watched closely. There it was decided to call a general council at a place called Council Grove. This grove was quite well known at that time, being a meeting ground of the naked, or Plains Indians, and the timber, or Eastern Indians; it was west of what now is Oklahoma City. It was decided that the Shawnee families should leave their settlement one at a time, ostensibly to go on a long hunting expedition. Each family was to go in a different direction, as if not expecting to go together, but all were to meet at a given time at Council Grove.

I was about two years old when my father took his family and left our home as if going on a hunting expedition. He took a few ponies and some of the necessary belongings of the family, but left the major part of his property, consisting of hogs, a few cattle, some farming implements, and a growing crop of corn. My mother had fifty head of horses that had been given her by her mother, and only a few of them could be taken. In due time, after certain maneuvers to dispel suspicion, my father with his family headed for Council Grove, arriving, as did the others, at the appointed time.

CIVIL WAR DAYS

II

COUNCIL GROVE was a wide strip of heavily wooded land situated at the edge of a prairie country, and contained ample facilities for camping. The timber offered a cool shade in the heat of summer, and provided a windbreak for the cold winds of winter; there was plenty of wood for fires, and a spring of clear, cold water. The place was known among the Indians all over the country, both east and west.

When my father and his tribesmen reached Council Grove they found several other tribes already encamped there. A band of runaway Negroes were there too, hiding in the grove. The slaves had run away from their masters, in different parts of the country, and had gathered there hoping to hide from searching parties who were scouring the country. These escaped slaves told horrible stories about slavery, declaring they would rather die than return to their masters. These tales interpreted to the Indians helped them decide which side of the controversy between the states they should take.

While they were pondering over what course they should pursue, a group of Confederate soldiers, mostly Creek Indians, appeared and demanded that the Shawnees return with them. The Shawnees refused and were upheld in this refusal by other tribes gathered there. The Confederates being hopelessly outnumbered returned without a fight. But our people realized that they only had been given a

[9]

respite, that the Creeks believed the Shawnees owed it to them to join the Confederacy, and would make another attempt to gain their end. The Shawnees and many others lost no time in getting away. My father and his family were among this number; they went north into Kansas.

I can remember something of this journey. I remember the wide prairie country we traveled through, with not a tree in sight. I remember one place we camped, where mother could not find anything with which to build a fire to cook our food. There were no brush or sticks, not even weeds that she could burn. But finally she succeeded in building a fire of dried buffalo manure—called buffalo chips—which was plentiful and burned well. The men killed some buffalo too, and we had plenty of meat, and of course the skins were saved, for they were considered of great value, being useful for many purposes. This trip must have taken a long time for it was early in the year 1863 when we finally reached the Shawnee settlement near Bellmont, Kansas. There the grass was fine for our horses, and fish and game were plentiful for our food.

Our principal chief, Jim Squire (Indian name Pay-low-es-tha, meaning flying afar), went on farther into Kansas to consult with the Shawnee Chief Black Bob and his band, and to ask their advice about what our people should do.[1]

1. To understand the division in the Shawnee tribe, and the location of the different bands or groups one must be familiar with the general history of the tribe or nation.

The original home of this once large and powerful tribe was in what now is Kentucky and Tennessee. From there they went forth in bands or groups in war or on hunting expeditions, often remaining away for many months or even years. There are records of treaties being made with bands or clans in widely separated sections of the country. No doubt there were slight disagreements and jealousies among the different clans, but their tribal organization was a strong one, and they always held councils together when questions of importance affected the tribe as a whole.

Evidently a disagreement took place shortly before the War of the Revolution which caused a permanent division of the tribe into two factions, each headed by a

When our chief reached the village where Chief Black Bob lived he was warmly received and welcomed by the Shawnees living there. Chief Black Bob and a number of his people returned with Chief Jim Squire, and stayed with us visiting during the winter. No doubt all tribal differences were forgiven and forgotten, and there was much feasting and story-telling, as these two powerful leaders related the experiences of their different bands during all the years the tribe had been separated. It is interesting to note that al-

---

chief from one of the two principal clans, the Tha-we-gi-la and the Cha-lah-gaw-tha. The band under the leadership of the Tha-we-gi-la chief went into New Spain and the Spanish government granted them a tract of land twenty-five miles square near Cape Girardeau (now Missouri). The remainder of the tribe under the leadership of the Cha-lah-gaw-tha chief remained in the region of the Ohio River, little groups of them being scattered over a large area. A large group was located in Ohio, and they took part in several wars or raids against the white settlers of that region.

The Shawnee historians declare that the group to which the Spanish government granted land at Cape Girardeau suffered another division, when the majority of them went into the Mexican country, and settled about what now is Menco, Texas. The Mexican government granted them this land and after the Texas-Mexican War the Republic of Texas recognized their claim.

But after Texas was admitted into the United States—the Shawnee historians claim—soldiers went to the homes of the Shawnees and loaded their household goods into wagons, and drove away. The soldiers probably explained their actions, but the Indians could not understand. They followed the wagons that held their goods. When they reached the southern boundary of the Indian Territory the soldiers unloaded the Indians' goods in little heaps on the ground, and gave $100.00 to each head of a family, and left them.

The Indians took what they could of their household effects and went farther into the Indian Territory until they came to the Creek country. The Creeks and the Shawnees had been friendly before either tribe moved into the western country, and now the Creeks welcomed the homeless Shawnees into their territory.

In the meantime those who had been left to occupy the land at Cape Girardeau entered into a treaty with the United States government in 1825 and exchanged their land at Cape Girardeau for land on the Kansas River, west of the state of Missouri. Later (in the year 1832), the government admitted the Ohio Shawnees to the land already granted the other group without their consent. Those who were absent were not notified or consulted in any way, though in one treaty there was a limited provision made for "the Absent Shawnees." However those who were absent never were notified of the fact. It was from this treaty that the name "Absentee Shawnees" was established for the group headed by the chief of the Tha-we-gi-la clan, this being the band to which Mr. Alford's family belonged.

[11]

though the two bands had been separated for more than fifty years each had held so tenaciously to their creeds, customs, and traditions that neither had changed at all. They took up their life together with no jar or discord and again they were an undivided people.

Chief Black Bob advised our chief to have his people remain in the region of Bellmont, for the reasons already given and for another very important one, which was that no whisky was sold there.

Chief Black Bob died the following spring.

Although our people had successfully avoided taking part in the war while they were with the Creeks, they were unable to resist the pressure brought to bear upon them after they went into Kansas. Perhaps the younger men relished the thought of a real fight, having heard so many interesting stories of warfare in earlier days. Many of our young men enlisted in Company M, Fifteenth Kansas Cavalry. My father was among this number. He became a sergeant in his company, and served until the close of the war. I still have his discharge paper with me.

I can remember quite well an incident that happened while my father was in the army. One day an Indian soldier, a Shawnee relative of ours, came home on a furlough. He brought a large bundle to my mother, saying that my father had sent it to her. We children were eager to see what the bundle contained, but mother waited until the soldier had gone before she opened the package. It was a big blue overcoat, such as the Union soldiers wore. Mother proceeded to rip the sleeves out at the shoulder seam and turn them into leggings for me. They proved to be too long, but I turned them up at the bottom, and was the proudest little chap on earth, as I strutted about, the envy of all the children in the settlement. Our clothing at that time consisted of a long shirt and leggings, with moccasins in the winter. The leggings were made of heavy woolen goods or leather. The moccasins were made by mother of hide she tanned herself. In summer we wore only the shirt. Mother made the rest of the great coat into clothing for the other children—there were three of us then. After a day or two the soldier who was returning to his post came by to see if mother had a message to send father, and saw me with the beautiful blue leggings on, and laughed heartily. He then dubbed me "soldier," and from that day on, I was known among my young companions as "soldier." It was the first English name I was given, and I was very proud of it. I bore this name—as a nickname—until I started to school, when I was about twelve years old.

After the close of the Civil War there was a great flood of immigration to the West. Kansas had come in for a great deal of favorable advertisement because of the stand the people had taken against slavery, and a great many people flocked there to take up land. Special inducement was offered to former soldiers in the way of homesteads. The government began to look about for a place to move some of the Indian tribes who held reservations in the more desirable sections of the country. The different tribes held councils and entered protests, all to no avail. The land was needed for white settlers, and the Indians must be moved.

After considerable protest the Shawnees agreed to a proposal that was made whereby they hoped to settle for all time everything pertaining to their land and property. Their chief, John White, entered into a treaty whereby the Absentee Shawnees were to be moved to the Indian Territory and allowed to select for themselves any land that was not already apportioned to another tribe. This treaty of 1867 was never ratified, therefore does not appear in government

[13]

records. It was not for want of merit that this treaty was not ratified, but because of some powerful interest against it. [2]

Our people returned to the Indian Territory when I was about eight years old, and in time were located in what is now Pottawatomie County, Oklahoma. Some of the people settled on the north bank of Little River, at the place where the Santa Fe railroad crosses the river. There they located one of their dance grounds, which always was a nucleus for a village or settlement. Others settled down the river, toward the Seminole country, while still others encamped in the timber near what now is the southwest corner of Tecumseh, where a dance ground also was placed. Others settled over the highlands of the North Canadian River valley, from which they later selected and moved upon their permanent locations, where their homes are today. Some of these early locations are indicated by little squares for houses and small scratches for fields on the original map of the United States survey made in 1872-1873.

It must be remembered that moving was a simple matter for our people in those days, though often it was a prolonged journey. Sometimes we camped in a locality for weeks or even months, waiting for floods to subside, or for one reason or another that suited the fancy of our leaders. Sometimes

2. The treaty with the Absentee Shawnees made in 1867, whereby they were to return to the Indian Territory and select their reservation on any land that was not already occupied or claimed by some other tribe, was never ratified, therefore does not appear among the Senate Documents. The Shawnees selected for their reservation land that the government had purchased from the Seminole Indians for the purpose of settling small tribes that had to be removed from the states. Later when the government arranged with the Pottawatomie tribe to leave their reservation in Kansas and take up land in Indian Territory the land that had been taken by the Absentee Shawnees was allotted to them, because there was no record showing it to be occupied. When the Pottawatomies arrived in the country they believed themselves to be the rightful owners of the land, and there was much bitter feeling between the two tribes. It was not until the final allotment of homesteads before Oklahoma was opened for white settlement that the matter was settled to the satisfaction of both tribes.

a crop of corn was planted and harvested before a journey was resumed. There was no cause for hurry; no business waited for our attention; no appointments had to be kept. Our homes, *we-gi-was* or cabins, could be built in a few days, and often were abandoned with little concern. We had little in the way of household effects: few clothes, a few buffalo robes, blankets, a few cooking vessels, and the crude and limited supply of utensils and implements used in carrying on the work about the camp. There were few wagons. The family effects generally were tied in bundles and strapped on the backs of horses—some were carried by the women. There was conversation and often merriment, as the groups tramped along through woods or prairie, over mountains or hills and boggy swamps. Streams were forded and when too deep or swift to wade, rafts were made to ferry across.

Our people lived at that time principally on game and corn. Sometimes beans and pumpkins were planted. As I have already stated most of the labor was done by the women—with very few exceptions—even the building of our homes or we-gi-was.[3] The building of the we-gi-was was the cause of much friendly rivalry for it took a peculiar skill and dexterity to construct them properly. They were waterproof and afforded far more comfort in extremely cold weather than one would think, from a cursory glance. Constructed as they were without the use of a hammer, a saw, or nails, they mutely testified to the neatness and pride of their owners and builders, even as do the homes of the

3. The English word "wigwam" is taken from the Indian word we-gi-wa which was used to designate the home or abode of the Indians of the East, or timbered country. Some writers used the word lodge in the same sense. The we-gi-wa, or wigwam, or lodge is fixed, not movable, made in oblong or square form like a house; they are made of bark or hides or woven mats with vertical walls and sloping roof. The word teepee is the name given to the abode of the naked, or Plains Indians of the West. A teepee is a movable tent of hides, rush mats, or cloth, built in a conical shape upheld by poles brought together at the top and tied securely.

working people of today. To build a we-gi-wa (which generally was made of the bark of an elm tree, though there were other trees from which the bark could be used), a tall, slender tree without low limbs was selected. The bark was severed all around the tree near the ground, with an ax or other sharp implement, then it was cut in the same way above, as high as could be reached; the bark then was cut through, straight down from the higher circle to the lower one. Into the opening thus made was inserted a flat wedge-shaped end of a hard stick prepared and seasoned for this purpose, with which the bark was pried off and open in a wide sheet. This was easily accomplished in spring and summer, when sap was in the trees. Then the bark was laid flat on level ground, with flesh side under, weighted down with small logs, and allowed to dry to a certain extent, but used while still soft and pliable. Then poles were cut of straight young trees and set into the ground at regular distances apart, outlining the size desired for the we-gi-was. All bark was peeled off the poles to keep worms from working in it. Two of these poles with a fork at the top of each were set at opposite ends and at half way the width of the we-gi-wa. Upon these forks were laid the ends of a long pole, lengthwise with the we-gi-wa, and tied securely thereon with strips of rough bark. This formed the top comb of the roof, to which the rest of the poles were bent at a suitable height for the walls and firmly secured there with strips of bark. Then upon and across these were laid other poles at regular distances from the top comb, down the slope to the end of the roof, and on down the sides to form walls. Upon these cross poles were laid the sheets of bark to close the roof and walls, securely held in place by other poles laid on the outside of the bark and tied fast to the poles within. The work seems intricate and would be to a novice but to a dexterous Indian woman of sixty years ago, it was easily and quickly done.

Some of our people made their beds in somewhat the same manner, by driving four forked sticks into the ground, in a square or oblong size, and upon these were laid two strong long poles that were a support to other shorter poles laid crosswise and all securely tied, making a firm, smooth support for bedding. Others, not so industrious, merely spread their bedding upon brush laid upon the ground floor of their we-gi-was. There were other contrivances made by the ingenious housekeeper, such as shelves, benches, and tables. Extra clothing and other supplies were hung from the poles that served as rafters, in neat or haphazard ways according to the taste of the housewife.

INDIAN CHILD LIFE

III

IT WAS about the year 1868 when my father and mother with other members of their tribe returned to the country then known as the Indian Territory where they had been told to select their permanent home. For eight years they had wandered from place to place with no settled home, but their family had increased. Often we had slept on the ground, with no roof to cover us. Our food had been scarce many times, yet our family life had gone on in its regular routine; the care and training of the children had been given just as much thought as if we had lived happily in an established community.

I believe many people will be surprised when told that Indian parents realized just as much responsibility for the training of their young as any other race of people. In fact I now believe that the Indian family of fifty years ago paid more attention to the teaching of their children than does the average white family of today. There were no schools, no paid teachers, but race pride and ambition was stronger then than now.

Indians were considered heathen, but each tribe held to some kind of religion or faith of its own. We believed in the existence of a Supreme Being whom we designated as Mo-ne-to, who ruled the universe, dispensing blessings and favors to those who earned His good will, and whose frown or disfavor brought unspeakable sorrow to those whose conduct merited His ill will: The Great Spirit, or ruler of destinies was believed to be a Grandmother who was constantly weaving an immense net which was called Ske-mo-tah, and it was the Shawnee belief that when the great net was finished it would be lowered to the earth, and all would be gathered into its folds who had proven themselves by their actions to be worthy of the better world, the happy hunting ground. The world then would come to an end, and some horrible fate awaited those who were left. (The pronoun *he* is used in speaking of the Great Spirit because there is no feminine gender in the Shawnee language. Men and women are spoken of as of the same gender, only the name of the individual contains the discrimination. Personal pronouns are neither masculine nor feminine, and most of them are mere affixes to other words.)

The Shawnee people had their own religious beliefs and convictions. Children were taught that good conduct would earn a reward and evil conduct would bring sorrow; from early childhood this principle was instilled into their minds. Standards of conduct were just as rigid as the laws of any other people, but force seldom was used to enforce good conduct. *Each person was his own judge.* Deceitfulness was a crime. We lived according to our own standards and principles, not for what others might think of us. Absolute honesty towards each other was the basis of character. They knew nothing of what the white race calls "good breeding" and they had never heard of the "Golden Rule" but both principles were embodied in their intercourse with each other. They expressed it in their language in the following form.

"*Tagi nsi walr mvci-lutvwi mr-pvyaci-grlahkv, xvga mytv inv gi mvci-lutvwv, gi mvci-ludr-geiv gelv. Walv uwas-panvsi inv, wa-ciganv-hi gi gol-utvwv u kvgesakv-namv manwi-lanvwawewa yasi golutv-mvni geyrgi.*

"*Tagi bemi-lutvwi walr segalami mr-pvyaci-grlahkv, xvga mvtv inv gi bemi-lutvwv, gi bemi-ludr-geiv gelv. Wakv vhqalami inv, xvga nahfrpi Moneto ut vhqalamrli nili yasi vhqalamahgi gelv!"*

The translation of which is as follows:

"Do not kill or injure your neighbor, for it is not him that you injure, you injure yourself. But do good to him, therefore add to his days of happiness as you add to your own.

"Do not wrong or hate your neighbor, for it is not him that you wrong, you wrong yourself. But love him, for Moneto loves him also as He loves you!"

Thus we are taught that to do wrong is a kind of boomerang to the evildoer, and these principles were followed, generally, by even the most ignorant of our people. If this spirit was lacking in their intercourse with other races, who can say it was not justified? If cunning and deception were resorted to in dealings with white people, it was pitted against something that the red man felt powerless to cope with on a common ground—something for which he had no name. If some of our beliefs were based on superstition, it must be acknowledged that they were not unlike the teachings of Christianity. The main point of difference is that our people believed *they only were responsible for their conduct towards their own race*, especially their own tribe, or others who were kind to them. To the white man they owed nothing, except to return in kind the treatment they received.

The training and teaching of the young then, formed an important part in the lifework of our people, and was not neglected even though the family had no fixed place of abode nor established household regulations. Men did not leave the training of their sons to their wives, as so many do today. In fact I believe that the men of our race take a greater interest in the training of their sons than do the white men with whom I have been associated. White men generally leave the moral training of their children to their wives, but pride of offspring is one of the strongest factors in the lives of our people. Every Indian father taught his sons those things he considered essential for him to know; every Indian mother sought to instill into her daughter's mind lessons she would never forget. Nothing was left to a public teacher or to chance; a parent felt his responsibility keenly.

To begin with, children were taught to respect their elders, not only their own parents, but all who were even beginning to show an advance in years; this virtually means respect for authority. It often is observed that Indians take to institutional training better than white children; they make good soldiers, observe rules and discipline scrupulously. This is because they are bred to respect authority; they obey without question.

All of our lessons had to be learned from our elders; all of our histories, traditions, codes, were passed from one generation to another by word of mouth. We had no books, no printed language, no written rules. Our memories must be kept clear and accurate, our observation must be keen, our self-control absolute.

Indian parents gave few commands, because they were advocates of freedom of action and thought, but absolute obedience was exacted. Children seldom were punished, for a few words of praise from a parent or an elder was regarded as the highest prize that could be given for good conduct. A child would strive with all his might to win such praise, while he would be indifferent to bodily punishment. However there were times and conditions when punishment was resorted to in order to impress some lesson on an erring youth. One punishment that was always a bitter one to an Indian child was to have some of his faults told to a visitor or friend. In cases when a severe punishment was deemed necessary, children's thighs and calves of their legs were scratched with a *la-lah-so-waw-ka*, an implement kept for this purpose, made by piercing a block of soft wood with pins or hard thorns about one-eighth of an inch apart, with the thorns or pins protruding on the reverse side. The instrument itself was about one and one-half inches wide. This was a very painful punishment and one that was seldom used. Sometimes parents used switches or sticks to beat their children, and that was considered a disgrace, to both the parent and the child.

Indian children of those days were as healthy as little animals, and even in their play did those things that developed their bodies and strengthened their muscles. Running, swimming, and jumping were matters of course with us, but the older men encouraged us to practice those things that developed greater strength; also they taught us to shoot our bows and arrows with accuracy and great skill.

A favorite game when a group of boys played together was one that taught skill in shooting at moving objects. A round hoop was made of a wild grapevine bent around until the ends lapped a little, then tied securely with strips of bark. It was then woven closely with pliable bark, making a thick, strong, smooth hoop. The boys would "choose sides," even as white boys do when playing games, and stand in two lines, facing each other fifteen or twenty feet apart. One of the boys would roll the hoop along on the ground, and the boys on the opposing side would shoot at it with their bows and arrows as it passed. The boy whose arrow stuck into the hoop was a winner; then the boys of the opposing side stuck their arrows into the ground and the winner tossed the hoop flatwise to the row of arrows to knock them down. As many as he succeeded in knocking down became his own. This game was something like the game of "keeps" which I see small boys playing with marbles today.

We had a game that we played with smooth, round stones, or we sometimes found peach seeds or stones which we whittled into balls that we used in a game like marbles as played by white boys. We played ball too, but our game was not like the baseball of today. All the games we played were calculated to develop strength, skill, and resourcefulness. The only toys we had were those we ourselves made. We wrestled and ran races and rode the ponies, fished and hunted, and set traps for birds and rabbits.

Indian girls never were allowed to play with the boys. In fact from the time a little Indian boy could walk he felt a sense of superiority to his sisters, and a boy who would have played with a girl was a subject for ridicule. Little girls played much as little girls do today, I suppose, mimicking their mothers' household tasks, making cakes, and molding vessels of mud or clay. No doubt they "kept house" and mothered the smaller children, even as I have seen my own little girls doing in recent years.

Our people appreciated skill or knowledge of any kind, and encouraged any young man or boy who showed evidence of a keen mind to develop his talents, but naturally they thought more of the wisdom that formed the background of our own racial life. The knowledge of warfare, of history, and of nature, to know the habits of wild creatures, to know about trees, wild plants and fruits, to be able to judge of weather, to foretell what the seasons would be, whether a cold winter or a dry summer—there were signs one might learn to read all these things by—all these things constituted a well-rounded education for the average young Indian man. All these things called for a good memory, keen observation, and close application, and with these gifts one naturally would learn much in other fields. Endurance and self-control were taught so rigidly that those qualities had become a part of Indian character. It was a proud and

[23]

happy day when an Indian boy realized that his father considered him old enough to begin actual training.

I remember as if it were yesterday, the day when father said to mother, in his soft Shawnee tongue, "Gaynwah is getting a big boy," and a knowing smile passed between them that was not lost on my understanding. I drew myself up to my full height and walked about among the other children with conscious pride, for very well I knew that father had some special meaning in those words. A few days later when the first frost had fallen, early in the morning my father spoke to me.

"Gaynwah, take off your shirt and run down to the creek and jump into the water."

It made me shiver to think of the cold plunge, but I never thought of disobeying him, for very well I knew that father had begun to train me to be a man, a brave—possibly a chief. Pride filled my heart! I did as father had told me, the other children looking on with admiration and respect. Every morning during that winter I repeated that performance, breaking the ice when it was necessary.

After several weeks father considered that I was ready for another test, so one morning he told me I should jump into the creek four times instead of one. On the fourth time I came up out of the water I should grasp something in my hand—just anything that should happen to come in contact with my hand in the water. It might be a leaf from a tree, a horse hair, a shell, or just any object—but whatever it was it would indicate my *o-pah-wa-ka* which would be a divine direction, for through that source I should receive some blessing from the Great Spirit, some power to perform worthy acts, that would guide me through life. I was not to open my hand after closing it under the water, until I stood before father. I did as I was instructed, but I failed to get anything in my hand, which was interpreted to mean that

I should earn my blessing in some other way, by worthy actions.

Another test of endurance for boys was given me when I was about ten years old. When a boy got up in the morning his face was blacked with charcoal, and he was sent out to kill some game for food. It might be a quail, a rabbit, or a squirrel, seldom larger game than that. He was given no food until he returned with what he was sent out to procure. Because his face was blacked everyone who saw him knew why he was out, and no one gave him food or helped him in any way. Unaided he must find what he had gone out to kill. He was absolutely on his own resources. Sometimes it was found in a few minutes or a few hours. More often it took long hours of searching and wandering —just a matter of luck. It took me two days to kill the quail my father had sent me out to bring home. Quail was plentiful then, but I just could not kill one with my bow and arrow, it seemed. After wandering for hours without food, my aim was not steady, and there is something in feeling that so much depends on one's efforts—that a test is being made. But at last my arrow brought one down, and I retraced my steps homeward.

Oh, the joy, the pride that filled one's heart when he returned home victorious to a waiting and watching family! An Indian boy automatically went on with his own training after such tests as I have described, encouraged and urged on by his father, his friends, and members of his social clan.

SOME EARLY ADVENTURES

IV

DURING those early years of my life when our family wandered from place to place beyond the line of civilization, living in forests or on some river bank, in Indian villages or settlements, I do not remember seeing any white people. But as we sat around the campfire at night I heard a great many stories of white people, stories of wars, of deceptions and encounters that were not any more conducive to a feeling of trust and confidence in the white race than were the stories told to white children at that time of Indians and their treachery and warfare. As a boy I held just as much fear in my heart of a white man, as any white boy held fear of a "wild Indian." And just as the white boy had a curiosity to see an Indian (if he were safe and protected by his father), I had a burning desire to see a white man or a white boy.

Quite well do I remember the first white man I ever saw. He impressed me with a terrible fear and awe at first sight. But owing to his pleasant manner and friendly way of talking to father, I soon changed, and fear of him left me, though I did not understand one word that he said. However this feeling was towards him only, not towards the white race in general.

When we first came back to Indian Territory after our long sojourn in Kansas, father camped on Little River in what now is Pottawatomie County, for the winter. There was thick timber about the camping place to break the wind, plenty of fish in the stream, squirrel and other game abounded in the timber, and a fine crop of nuts was on the pecan trees, thus assuring him of food for the winter. Indeed it was a good place to live during the winter, but in the spring we moved further north where the country was open and the land easier to cultivate, and there we lived until a crop of corn was grown and harvested.

It was while we were living there, waiting for our corn to ripen that I saw the white man whom I mentioned. He was a licensed Indian trader who had opened a store near where we lived and sold many useful commodities to the Indians and bought and shipped the furs they trapped along the river. His name was McDonald, but the Indians called him Mac.

Near us lived three other Shawnee families: one was named Bullfrog, another Sampson, and the third was that of Robert Deer who spoke English quite well and was for many years interpreter for the Shawnees, later being employed as interpreter by the government. He was an intelligent man, and we children loved to hear him talk. He had traveled a good deal and had a store of interesting stories to tell.

I often played with the children of these families, and we used to go with our parents to Mac's store and gaze in wonder at the many interesting things he displayed. He always was very kind to us, and we learned not to fear him. Once when I was there with my father who had taken some skins to sell, Mac gave me a striped shirt which captivated my fancy entirely.

The first "store shoes" that I ever wore came from that store, and very well I remember how proud I was of them. It was after our crop of corn was harvested, that first year after we returned from Kansas. Father had settled on some land and started his homestead, which was on the North

Canadian River near the present site of the city of Shawnee. Father being more thrifty than some members of his tribe had accumulated a small herd of hogs that fed and fattened on the heavy mast, pecans, and acorns which grew in abundance on the rich bottom land. When we moved to the new home the hogs had to be herded and guarded until they grew accustomed to the changed location and became domesticated. This duty was assigned to my younger brother Dave and me. The land was overgrown with briars and thorny shrubs which scrached our feet and legs until they bled. We had a bad time keeping the hogs together. Then father went to Mac's store and bought us each a pair of boots. They were big and clumsy with brass tips on the toes but we were very proud of them. We tramped about enjoying the possession of our boots so much that we forgot all about the hogs which scattered about the woods. Father had great difficulty in finding them all. He threatened to take our boots from us if we neglected our work again, and we were more careful after that but still very proud of our boots.

After we had settled on this land we really felt that we owned our home. For the first time we had a house really built of hewn logs. Father and mother cleared and cultivated some land, and father bought some young apple trees from a white man who represented a nursery in Arkansas, and started an orchard. We had plenty of corn, meat, pumpkins, and beans, which meant plenty in those days. Father sold a few skins and hides occasionally and bought useful things from the store for the family. I can remember how proud and happy the family was. Our domestic and family life assumed a more regular routine. We felt secure in the possession of our home and land, in the promise of the government that it would never be taken away from us. There was abundance of grass for our horses, a good range for our hogs. We had many of the comforts of civilization, and we were content.

We used to hobble our horses by tying their feet together so they could not walk far or fast, and let them out to eat grass. Sometimes we would put a bell on the leader, for a drove of horses would always have one who was a leader, even as men are prone to follow one who assumes an air of authority. When we needed a horse to work or to ride we would herd the drove into a corral, catch those we needed, and then turn the others out to eat grass; thus they rustled their own feed.

One day one of the boys from the Sampson family came to our place and asked me to go with him to drive up their horses, saying that he would in turn help me to bring our horses home. He was riding a horse that just had been "broken," which means that it had not been ridden or taught to carry anyone on its back until about that time, or trained to be guided by its bridle. It had not been broken to carry double at all, but we decided that would be a good time to teach it that trick. I mounted behind the Sampson boy and to our surprise the horse offered no objection, and behaved very well for a time. Then he seemed suddenly to realize that he was being imposed upon. Perhaps he resented the too intimate touch of my heels in his flanks and began to pitch. Harder and harder the maddened horse plunged and pitched. Tighter and tighter I clamped my legs to his sides as the horse strove to free himself from the burden upon his back. Presently he gave a tremendous plunge that caught me unaware. I found myself flying through the air, then landed several feet from my partner who also had been thrown to the ground. I had a strange dazed feeling as I tried to rise; my left arm hung helpless at my side. It was broken. The other boy was stunned from his fall, but suffered no serious injury.

I felt no pain just at first, but as I took hold of my arm with my other hand, it began to pain me. I was scared, frantic, and made the woods ring with my howls as I hurried home to mother. Mother examined my arm, and shamed me for making such a noise, appealing to my manhood to endure the pain quietly. Then she made me as comfortable as she could while she hastened to prepare a bandage, for which she was known to be very skilful. Mother went to the creek near our house and cut a limb about the size of my arm from an elm tree, then quickly and dexterously she slipped the bark from the limb and placed it about my broken arm. She pulled the bone into place, adjusted it carefully, and bound the bark comfortably close about it with a skill that seldom is used except by professional surgeons. I was kept quiet, given plenty of cold water to drink until the fever had passed, and in due time my arm was healed perfectly.

After this sad experience, when I was perfectly well again father gave me a pony of my own which I named Puc-ki-may (mosquito) and which I loved very dearly.

I remember the first big game I ever killed. Early one morning I took father's long rifle and started out on my pony for a day's hunting. I went in a northeast direction for about five miles after crossing the North Canadian River. I stopped in a grove of trees that stood on the edge of a prairie. Sitting on my pony, scanning the horizon in every direction I saw presently that which I hoped to see— an enormous deer trotting towards me from the north, evidently utterly unaware of my presence. I jumped off my horse, tied him to a tree, and ran rifle in hand toward the deer. The tall blue-stem grass reaching about my head hid me from the deer who was coming swiftly in my direction, at intervals lowering his head to the ground as if trailing the herd to which he belonged. I reached a tree against which I could lean my rifle, and when the deer was the right distance from me, I gave a short sharp whistle—which my father had taught me to do, to attract the attention of the deer. The buck stopped instantly, his magnificent head raised to listen—I took careful aim and fired. To my great surprise and disappointment the buck leaped about, turned, and ran up a steep hill with such glorious leaps that I thought I had failed to hit him. I had expected him to fall dead when I fired; instead he ran off! But soon he turned to my left into an open prairie which gave me a clear sight of him, and oh joy! There close to his heart was a red spot; evidently I had aimed well. Just as I had reached this decision he gave another great leap, and fell. Down went my gun and I ran to him as fast as my legs would carry me. I was breathless when I reached him, but it was a wonderful sight to me. He seemed to be dead, and in my great joy I did not know what to do, so I grabbed him by his hind legs. But again he surprised me, for with one tremendous kick he sent me ten feet, where I landed on my back, but that was his death struggle.

It was still early in the day, and I began at once to skin the buck. Then I cut the venison into pieces so I could lift them and load them on my pony. I took almost every bit of that deer home with me, not forgetting his splendid head. It was late in the evening when I had finished, and quite dark when I reached home. To say that I was proud of my feat, and that my family received me joyfully, is hopelessly inadequate to express our sentiments on that occasion.

During the early years of my life, our people had a great deal of trouble with horse thieves. We lived near what was known as the "Abilene Trail," a broad open road or trail that was used by cattlemen from Texas in driving great herds of cattle to Kansas City and other markets. The Abilene trail ran directly from Abilene, Texas, and merged with the Chisolm Trail, a nationally known road that crossed the country from east to west, about forty miles north of our settlement.

A great many men of different classes, some outlaws fleeing from justice, others restlessly seeking adventure, passed over this trail, and as always the Indians were the targets for their villainy. There were no laws to control these men, and the Indians had no redress for their wrongs. The only means the Shawnees employed or could employ was a fight. If their horses were stolen they tried to overtake the thief, or thieves, and if they could not get their property from the thieves—then there was a fight.

I remember several such cases that occurred in my early boyhood when both white men and Indians were killed but I shall not dwell on that now. However I would like to say that I believe a great many of the stories of Indian cruelty of those days were results of such conduct as I have mentioned. Our people could not see things then, with the calm reasoning knowledge we have now. When they suffered an injury, they could retaliate only in their own way, and naturally they knew no reasoning except their own.

But our own experience with horse thieves was confined to one occasion. We had one horse that we prized very highly, named Sauk. He was a good horse for many purposes, but especially esteemed for riding. He seemed endowed with remarkable intelligence. No matter how black the darkness that might overtake one riding Sauk, away from home or just lost in the deep woods, just to let Sauk have the reins insured reaching home safely. Mother never worried when any of us were riding Sauk, for she knew he could be trusted to bring us home. But Sauk had one fault! That was a disposition to break loose when tied out. When staked out or tied up, after he grew tired of the place he would deliberately back, and hunch, and jerk, and pull until he would break the strongest rope, and he was free. This was an annoying habit, for we could not depend upon finding him, if left long in a place.

One night Sauk was stolen. We missed him early in the morning, and at once father and I took up the trail, for it was quite clear which direction the thief had taken, although he avoided the roads. We kept our horses on a trot most of the time, for evidently from the trail Sauk had trotted too, and the trail was clear. About the middle of the forenoon the trail turned north, and we crossed the North Canadian River at Keo-kuk Falls. We took no time to eat, but our horses drank at the river. We followed the thief all day, until darkness obscured the trail, and father and the horses were utterly tired out. We camped about five miles southeast of the Sauk and Fox Agency, staked out our horses, and ate our supper. Father was unusually silent as he sat smoking his pipe and seemed to be in deep thought, for Sauk was a valuable horse, and we could ill afford to lose him. We slept under a huge oak tree that night.

The next morning we rose at dawn, had a hurried breakfast, then father spoke to me, saying:

"Ni quetha" (my son), "we will return home. We cannot overtake our horse because the thief had too much the start of us. We will go to the Agency and have the Agent send notices where he thinks best."[1]

We went to the Agency, then returned home, traveling all day, and arriving home in the night, sad and disappointed. The next morning while we were eating our break-

1. When the Shawnee Indians returned to the Indian Territory they were placed under the jurisdiction of the Sauk and Fox Agency. It was the duty of the Indian Agent to look after such matters as the theft of a horse, or in fact anything pertaining to the welfare of the Indians under his care. All annuities were paid through the Agency, and all contracts the Indians made must be signed by the Agent to be considered legal or binding.

fast we heard a familiar neigh of a horse, and all ran out to see. There stood Sauk, with a short piece of rope about his neck, evidently as glad to be at home as we were to have him. No doubt he had left the thief afoot. We no longer considered Sauk's habit of breaking loose a fault.

INDIAN FOOD

V

AS CORN (rightly called Indian corn) was our staple food it may be interesting to note some of the methods of preparing it, for it was used in many ways besides that of making bread.

We had practically no storerooms, no cribs to hold our corn, because of the migratory habits of our people, and it took a good deal of ingenuity to keep a supply from one year's crop until another could be grown and harvested. The method generally used was that of stripping back the husks or shucks of the corn without breaking them off, and braiding them together securely in long ropes with the ears dangling. Those ropes were hung inside the cabins or we-gi-was, high up against the roof, when the family had no other storehouse. Much corn could be kept dry and sound in that way. Very few families raised enough corn to feed their horses over the winter, but there was always an abundance of hay, which with other green growth kept the animals in good condition.

Our people used several different varieties of corn, the seed of each kind being carefully preserved and kept separate from the other. Each kind of corn was especially desired for some particular food or dish.

From the time the corn was in the roasting ear state, it was a favorite food, and there were many ways of preparing it, both for present use and for storing it to be used after the season for fresh corn had passed. One favorite dish made from roasting ears was called *wes-ku-pi-mi* and was prepared in the following manner:

A ditch or trench was dug about one foot deep, a foot wide, and the length needed for the amount of corn to be cooked. The soil removed was piled at each end of the trench to serve as a support for two long poles of green wood, laid lengthwise of the trench. Before the poles were laid across the trench hickory wood was burned in it to make a bed of glowing hot coals. Then a row of carefully husked and trimmed ears of corn was stood on the ground on each side of the trench, with the tips of the ears resting against the green poles, and roasted. They were watched carefully and turned often so that the corn was thoroughly cooked, the grains toasted to a delicate brown. After they were thoroughly cooked and cooled, the grains were broken from the cobs with a blade made of bone or with a dull knife, and then dried in the sun. When dry they were carefully stored away for winter use. When it was to be eaten this corn was cooked in water. Sometimes meat was added for seasoning, making a delicious food. The rich flavor imparted by the hickory coals was especially liked.

Another way of preserving fresh corn with its peculiar delightful flavor was done by grating it from the cob, making a soft, milky mush which was then poured into an iron oven or baking kettle with a close fitting lid. It was baked very slowly and carefully until it became a solid cake. This was called *ne-pan-wi tak-u-wha* (production bread). When it was to be eaten it was prepared much as we prepare commercial cereals today.

There were several ways of preparing corn for food after it had become ripe and dry on the stalk. One of the most favored was called *tak-u-wha ne-pi* (bread water) by the Shawnees, and *afke* or *sofka* by the Muskogee Indians who must have taught it to the Shawnees, for it is generally called sofka, which is a Muskogee word. In this preparation the flinty variety of corn was used. The corn was brayed in a deep mortar with a pestle until the skin covering the grain was broken and separated from the kernels. It was then put into a broad, shallow, woven basket, called a *law-as-qah-thi-ka* (wafter) and wafted in the open air until cleaned of all skins or chaff. It was then boiled in water until the kernels were thoroughly cooked and it became a heavy whitish mass; more water was added, and a small quantity of seeping fluid—made by letting water seep through clean wood ashes—was added to the corn mixture. All was then poured into a large wooden vessel, covered, and set away until it fermented. Then it was ready for use and would keep indefinitely. It has a most pleasing taste, something like a sweet pickle, and was kept on hand in hospitable Indian homes and offered to visitors as a refreshing drink or food.

Another way of preparing ripe corn of the soft, starchy variety was somewhat as white people prepare hominy. The grains were boiled in water mixed with wood ashes until the skins would slip from the grains. Then the grains were washed in clear water until thoroughly free of skins. It then was cooked in a kettle, sometimes seasoned with meat, until the grains were very tender and soft. This was called *suh-day-wal-di* (swelled grains).

Another great delicacy that my mother often prepared was made of the flinty variety of corn and was called *osah-saw-bo* (viscid fluid). It was made in the same manner as tak-u-wha ne-pi, mentioned earlier, except that the seeping fluid was left out, and it was not allowed to ferment, but instead nut meats, walnuts, pecans, or hickory nuts were pounded and added to the corn, and all cooked together. It was a delicious food, and one that we especially enjoyed—nothing was equal to it.

[37]

As for our daily bread, our Indian women brayed ripe corn of the soft variety in a mortar until it was very fine. It was then sifted through a sieve, the coarser parts returned to the mortar and pounded again until a fine meal or flour was obtained. This was made into a dough with water (wheat flour was added when one had it), and baked in the iron kettle or deep oven with fitted lids on which hot coals were laid. Sometimes the cakes of dough were wrapped in several layers of clean corn husks which had been moistened, and buried in hot ashes to bake until thoroughly done. The delightful taste of bread baked this way cannot be described and is known now only to experienced campers.

Another way of preparing corn meal was called *gol-tha-wa-li* (emergency meal). This meal might be kept indefinitely—if kept perfectly dry—and was prepared in the same way as other meal, except that the grains of corn were thoroughly parched before being made into meal. This meal was kept by our people for use in an emergency, such as a sudden journey. It was an emergency ration of the warrior or the hunter, who never went away on a journey without a supply of this meal. It was very much condensed and was carried in a little bag, inside a larger bag of buckskin. A small quantity stirred into a cup of water made not only a good drink, but a nourishing meal in itself, and in an emergency would sustain one for many days, when no other food could be found.

There was another kind of bread we called *ske-pul-haw-na* (blue biscuit), made from meal. A small quantity of a peculiar kind of ashes was put into the meal, as is done with soda these days, and the meal then was made into a heavy dough with water. The dough was of a bluish color, and was molded by hand into a sort of three cornered biscuits that were dropped into a kettle of boiling water. When cooked they had a very pleasing flavor entirely their own, and were a deep blue color. They sometimes were dried and kept for future use, being reboiled when required. The ashes used to make blue biscuit were made by burning matured bean husks on a flat rock. They produced a pure white ash that was stored in bags by our women, and kept as we now keep soda.

At this point it may be interesting to note how our mothers made their sieves and other baskets used for culinary purposes, for it was done with a skill that now is a lost art. They obtained their material by cutting down a hackberry tree or an elm of the size they wanted. A section of the tree trunk clear of any defects or knots was chosen and carefully barked the desired length. The trunk selected then was pounded, gently but firmly and thoroughly, with a smooth flat edge of an ax. Every fraction of the surface received its gentle beating, until the layers of wood that represented the different years growth became loosened, and could be peeled from the trunk in narrow uniform strips in thin but strong, tough sheets. These strips were then woven into baskets, leaving the spaces between the strips tiny or larger, as was needed for the purpose of the basket. Some were woven so closely they would hold water, some were used for sifters for meal; others were used to grade grains of corn, letting all under a certain size pass through. Marvelous, the ingenuity of those women!

The making of those baskets was an arduous task, but baskets once made properly could be used for a long time. However, one of the commodities most eagerly sought after from the Indian traders was a white man's sifter.

As for other foods we had many kinds of meat in the olden time. Buffalo, deer, wild turkeys, ducks, and geese, as well as the smaller fowls such as prairie chickens, quail, and other small birds were abundant, but as the years passed and the country became more and more populous, game dwindled until a squirrel or an opossum became a rarity. When I was a boy, fish used to be plentiful in the streams, but now it is a lucky day when a small string of fish can be caught.

I want to say that for fine cooking of meat the women of my boyhood time had the best of it over the modern methods. Meat broiled over an open bed of coals has a juicy tenderness that cannot be equaled in the finest kitchen with its white enameled stove, and shining, polished surfaces. A duck or squirrel, wrapped in wet corn husks and baked or roasted in hot ashes, cannot be surpassed, according to my notion. Besides broiling and roasting over an open fire, meat was cooked in kettles, or baked in ovens when a rich gravy added to the pleasure of eating it. Beans and some corn dishes, as I have explained, were sometimes boiled with meat.

To boil meat two stout sticks three feet long with forked ends were driven into the ground some six or seven feet apart; another pole was laid in the forks of the sticks and kettles were swung from it over the bed of coals. Indeed this was the method used to roast meat, when a large piece was to be cooked. Swung from the pole, turned frequently, and the red hot coals kept at an even heat, meat acquired a tenderness and flavor that cannot be described. Moreover the odor that filled the air when meat was being cooked this way stimulated one's appetite more than the most costly sauces of today.

We had an abundance of wild fruit in season, such as wild strawberries, dewberries, blackberries, cherries, plums, and grapes. Papaws were abundant in some localities, and were a very delicious fruit when fully ripe. I believe they belong to the banana family. There were huckleberries on some hillsides; even the lowly persimmon was not despised, but highly valued for several reasons.

As a general thing we used fruit only when fresh, and just as picked from trees or bushes—seldom cooked. Our mothers had no preservatives to keep fruit or any cans to keep it fresh. However, fruits that could be dried were valued highly. For instance the persimmon was carefully cured. This fruit is very rich in sugar, and when freed from seed and a kind of fibrous core that gives it a puckery taste, is very good. From persimmons our mothers used to make a kind of cake that resembles a date cake of the present day, which was called *muc-hah-see-mi-ni tak-u-wha* (persimmon bread). To cure or dry persimmons they were first freed from seed and fibre. The remaining pulp was kneaded into oblong cakes of a uniform size, and then thoroughly dried in the sun. When needed for use it was freshened by steaming in hot water, or it was very palatable when eaten dry. Other fruits such as plums and berries were similarly prepared for drying, some being slightly baked before drying.

Mother use to make a dish that was a favorite with us all, called *psg-ib-haw* (sour food, which was a misnomer), that was delightful to my taste. Even to this day "Grandma Jenny" who is still with us, prepares it occasionally. It is made of wild grapes that are slightly scalded so the thick, rich juice may be pressed from the grapes. The juice then is heated, and while boiling, dumplings are dropped into it. Sugar was added to the juice—when we had it.

Sugar and syrup were made from sugar maple, but when our people were not in the country where sugar maple grew they substituted soft maple, box elder, and even hickory sap for the sugar maple sap, though of course the product was not so good. Sometimes a bee tree would be found with a priceless store of honey. My parents used to talk about the olden times when a great number of their people would gather together during the season when the sap was flowing in the sugar maple, and work together making sugar and syrup. Of course that was before they came to the Indian Territory, for real sugar maple doesn't grow in this part of the country.

As I look back over the years, and recall the hardships and privations endured by our people my heart aches with pity, then swells with pride, when I think how nobly they combatted the odds that were against them. Our mothers knew nothing of a balanced diet; they had never heard of calories or vitamins but they fed their families health and strength giving foods with an inborn wisdom. They had no markets to buy even the most ordinary foods. Delicacies and out-of-season vegetables and fruits were unheard of. But they relied upon their own industry, ingenuity, and skill to provide food and other necessities of life for their families, with never a complaint, and with a cheerfulness that should be an inspiration to the present generation. Little Indian children of that day and time were as healthy, and generally as happy, as little animals. It remained for civilization and the white man's system of living to breed discontent and to make invalids of a large number of our people.

TRIBAL GOVERNMENT

VI

MY FATHER, during the Civil War, contracted some kind of disease which attacked him occasionally and for several days after an attack he would be very ill and unable to care for himself. Because of this weakness and because I was the eldest son my mother sent me to accompany him on all his visits or hunting expeditions, so that I might care for him, or report to her should he become ill. Thus I was much in the company of my elders, and learned many things that ordinarily a boy of my age would not have known.

I learned while still young to see things from a man's point of view and to feel responsibility, not only for my father, but for the whole family and to a certain extent for our people. In fact the sense of care or responsibility that I felt for my father gave me a sober earnestness that must have seemed queer in a boy of my age. No doubt it was this seriousness that impressed the chiefs and leaders of our people so that they took more interest in me than they did in most boys of my age. While I still was very young they taught me many of the traditions and codes of our tribe. I never tired of listening to their stories, which rivalled ancient mythology in interest and beauty. Tribal history handed down from generation to generation by word of mouth is more fascinating than any fiction.

Originally there were five clans[1] composing the Shawnee tribe, including the two principal clans, Tha-we-gi-la and Cha-lah-kaw-tha, from one of which came the national or principal chief. The remaining three, the Pec-ku-we, the Kis-pu-go, and the May-ku-jay, each had its own chief who was subordinate to the principal chief in national matters, but independent in matters pertaining to the duties of his clan. Each clan had a certain duty to perform for the whole tribe. For instance the Pec-ku-we clan, or its chief, had charge of the maintenance of order and looked after the celebration of things pertaining to religion or faith; the Kis-pu-go clan had charge of matters pertaining to war and the preparation and training of warriors; the May-ku-jay clan had charge of things relating to health and medi-cine and food for the whole tribe. But the two powerful clans, the Tha-we-gi-la and the Cha-lah-kaw-tha,[2] had charge of political affairs and all matters that affected the tribe as a whole. Indeed, the tribal government may be likened to the government of the United States, in which each state (clan), with its governor (chief), is sovereign in local matters, but subordinate to the president of the United States (principal chief) in national matters. The difference is that the president of the United States must be elected, and may be changed with each election, while the principal chief came to his office by heritage and held it for life, or during good behavior.

At the time of which I write the Shawnee tribe had been divided for many years, and only the Tha-we-gi-la, the Pec-ku-we, and the Kis-pu-go clans were represented in the Absentee Shawnee band. These three clans always had been

1. The names of the five clans of the Shawnee tribe are preserved in Colonial history.

2. Chillicothe, Ohio, was named for the Shawnee clan Cha-lah-kaw-tha, or as it sometimes was spelled, Cha-lah-gaw-tha.

closely related, while the Cha-lah-kaw-tha and the May-ku-jay had always stood together, and were represented in the group that I have mentioned as living in Kansas at the time of the Civil War.

Besides the chiefs of the clans, there was a group of men in the tribe who made up the Council, which was composed of members of all the clans. The men on the Council were intelligent and staunch, fully able to advise about the affairs that affected the tribe. They took upon themselves much of the responsibility of governing it. My father was a member of the Council, and his associates were men of intelligence and wisdom. They discussed with deep concern subjects relating to the welfare of our people. They knew our own history and that of many other tribes as well. Their memories were excellent, and they could remember the gist of all the treaties our people had made with the government as they had been interpreted to them—for generations.

I find it a little difficult to explain the supremacy of the ruling class of the Shawnee tribe. Although we were absolutely democratic, believing that all men (that is, all Shawnee men) were born equal, we accorded to our leaders and chiefs a deference that was spontaneous. There was no vacillating between different leaders. Once a man established his reputation for bravery, for wisdom and discretion, he became an object of admiration and confidence. Those qualities could not be assumed—they must be inborn. An Indian is too close an observer to fail to recognize any false pretense. Our chiefs were aristocrats. They carried themselves with conscious pride. In fact they often were called "vain."

Each chief appointed his subordinates to distribute the work of his clan. Most appointments were made for life, but they usually contained the phrase "during good behavior." There was a dignity and courtesy in the manner of these men towards each other, even in their most intimate association, that I have found painfully lacking in the intercourse of many of the white men with whom I have been thrown. Believing that all natural things were sacred, there were no cheap or ribald jokes about the functions of nature.

Shawnee men were absolutely honest with each other. Towards others they might regard cunning or deceit as permissible, even as some white men maintain that "business is business, you know" when trying to excuse some of their transactions. Among Shawnee Indians this shade of dishonesty does not exist, or where it is found to exist, it is looked upon as a disgraceful crime. This honesty is demonstrated by the fact that when hunting, a deer, a wild turkey, or any game, no matter how highly valued or scarce it might be, could be left hanging in a tree with a piece of clothing or any sign to show ownership, and it never was molested. So it was with a bee tree, which was considered one of the richest treasures a hunter could find. Any mark of ownership would hold such a find until the owner or finder could come to take the honey or to carry home his game.

This brings to mind an incident which involves the principles of that great and mysterious word called "civilization," so mysterious in fact that I never have comprehended fully all that it includes. It is one of the lessons taught by those persons whom I have mentioned before as coming among us for no other reason than to prey upon our ignorance and simple honesty.

An intelligent member of the Pec-ku-we clan named Billy Axe had learned to speak and write a few words of English and was very proud of the accomplishment. One day while hunting in the woods Billy Axe found a fine bee tree. Thinking that would be a good opportunity to use some of his newly acquired knowledge he wrote on a card he had in his pocket, "This is my bee tree," and signed his name, then tacked the card on the tree, expecting to come back in a few days with proper vessels to take care of the honey. When he did go back prepared to take the highly prized delicacy, he found his tree cut, and all the precious honey gone. No Indian in the country could have read the words on the card, so he knew that a white man had taken it. Had he marked it in a manner known only to the Shawnees, he would have found his honey just as he had left it. Poor Billy Axe laid the whole matter against the paleface and his "civilization." Billy Axe's "bee tree" has been the source of many jokes among our people, even up to the present time.

As I went about with my father I learned at an early age many of those unwritten, undefinable rules that governed the intercourse of our people, and of the simple natural courtesy of Indian men towards each other. They were, it seems to me now, utterly devoid of envy, and the phrase "in honor preferring one another" appropriately could be applied to them. They upheld a strong moral tone and used their influence with the younger generation to prevent lawlessness. All recognized the evil and danger in strong drink and besought our young men to refrain from intoxicating liquor.

The responsibility placed upon the individual members of a clan for the good behavior of the whole is illustrated by an incident that I recall. There were several young fellows who associated together and formed the habit of getting drunk. They would ride on their ponies many miles to get liquor, and waste money their families needed, to buy it. A council was held to consider what should be done to stop them. The older men of the clan to which these young fellows belonged were instructed by their chief to talk to them and to warn them of the danger to their health, the detriment to their characters, and the possibility of getting into serious trouble. But the young fellows persisted in their evil ways.

Then a council of all the chiefs was called by the principal chief, and they were instructed to talk to the young men. This they did but to no avail. Then a general council was held of all the chiefs and all their people, including the culprits themselves, and the principal chief addressed the wrongdoers himself. After kindly but firmly telling them of the harm that would come to them if they persisted in doing evil, he turned to the assembly of people, many of them friends and relatives of the young men, and commanded them, each and every one of the Shawnee nation to take the matter into his own hands. Anyone who saw any of the young fellows in an intoxicated condition *was ordered to shoot him down as though he were an enemy.*

This order was effective, and the young men quit drinking, and became honorable, upright members of their tribe. Some of their descendants are living now, good, law abiding citizens.

The Shawnee Indians were the first body of people to advocate prohibition. According to Colonial records of Pennsylvania they first took action April 24, 1733, and requested Governor Gordon that "firm orders be sent to break into pieces all kegs of rum brought into their town." On May 1, 1734, they dictated a letter to the governor and his council, asking that no trader be allowed to bring more than thirty gallons of rum into their territory, and added that if more was brought they "would stave his kegs, and seize his goods."

Four years later, on March 20, they reported to the Council of Pennsylvania, that after holding a council they had concluded "to leave off drinking for four years; that they had staved and spilled all the liquor in their town belonging to both whites and Indians, which consisted of about forty gallons thrown into the streets." This report was accompanied by a pledge signed by ninety-eight Shawnees and two white traders agreeing that all liquors be spilled. Four men were appointed in each town to see that no rum be brought for the period of four years.

We had no officers, no prisons, but misdeeds did not go unpunished. Punishment was of many kinds, and was determined by the gravity of the offence. Our chief's word was law, and any persistent refusal to obey the acceptable but unwritten code of honorable conduct was punishable by severe flogging or even death. Anyone who refused to take his punishment like a man, was ostracized from his tribe, his friends, and his family—an extreme to which death was preferable.

Nor were the women of our tribe free from the law. The most heinous crime of which a woman could be convicted was that which we called *pock-wa-no ma-dee-way* (gossip about people). I remember hearing about a woman whose chief pleasure in life was the telling of stories of the baser side of human nature. Her name was *Waw-ki-wa-si* (Betsey Squirrel). She loved to talk about people, especially about other women.

Betsey Squirrel was warned to stop this pernicious habit, but she persisted. Finally the chief sent a committee of three men to thrash her with switches. Long Gibson, a six-foot fellow, had charge of the committee. Naturally the woman's husband objected to having his wife whipped. Two of the men took him in charge and held him until his wife's punishment was finished, then he too was thrashed. This woman was never known to be guilty again, and some of her descendants still are living in Pottawatomie County. Squirrel Creek, a small stream south of the city of Shawnee, was named for this family, their home being near its bank.

There was a story told by the Kickapoo Indians which was corroborated by our own people, who were familiar with the facts. The story was used as an illustration of the proper way to treat those who did not act honorably. Prior to the Civil War some Kickapoo Indians were located in the neighborhood of Benson Park and the present Shawnee Agency. There was a Kickapoo village on the very ground where the Benson Park baseball field now is located. In this village lived a young Indian named *Say-kaw-quah* (Skunk), who was not exactly honest and had a bad habit of giving his people trouble. Finally Say-kaw-quah committed some crime against the whites, who demanded his death.

The Kickapoo chiefs held a long council, and finally decided that they would have to comply with the demand, and slay the guilty man. His own relatives were required to kill him, which they did, and his head was sent to the white people who demanded his death. His body then was taken to a hill about three quarters of a mile away, and left there unburied.

After our return from Kansas in 1868 Skunk's bleached bones still were there and the place was called *Say-kaw-ku-gi* (place of the skunk). It was said by the superstitious Indians that Skunk always gave the Kickapoo war whoop just before a storm.

When my father settled on his land we lived only about a mile east of Say-kaw-ku-gi, and my brother Dave and I heard the story of the bleaching bones of the Skunk and went over to the hill to see them for ourselves. Sure enough they were there, just as we had heard they were, and we were thrilled with a superstitious awe and did not tarry long on the hill. Mother heard about our visit and forbade us to go there again.

Another story illustrating the reverence for tribal laws that all Indians felt was that of a Seminole Indian who was sentenced by a council of chiefs to be shot for some transgression. He was allowed the customary sixty days to attend to his family affairs and prepare to die. At the appointed time the doomed man took his coffin—which he had made himself—and drove to the place where he was to be executed. But to his surprise no executors were there to receive him. Patiently he waited three days, then along came some members of his tribe who told him that tribal government had been abolished, and under the new territorial laws his tribesmen had no authority to execute him. He returned to his mourning family and thriftily stowed his coffin in the loft of his cabin to be used when he died a natural death, which occurred eighteen years later.

I was so closely associated with my father from my earliest days until his death, accompanying him on his visits to the chiefs and headmen, listening to the discussions at council meetings, that I believe I was thoroughly familiar with the inmost working of the tribal government. I was acquainted with all the leaders and I knew well the full history of the tribe. I remember quite well our principal chief John White who died in 1872. Father and I with many others were present at his funeral. He was buried on the north bank of Squirrel Creek, a few hundred feet east of the present crossing of the Santa Fe Railroad, with an impressive funeral ceremony befitting his standing and station. After his death John Sparney became our principal chief, with "Uncle Joe" Ellis remaining second chief. My mother's brother, Big Jim, was chief of the allied Pec-ku-we and Kis-pu-go clans, with Sam Warrior as second chief.

THE WAY OF THE INDIAN

VII

A S I WENT about with my father and his associates I heard a great many discussions that were not favorable to the white man. Those men who carried the burden of responsibility for their people felt very keenly the change that they constantly saw taking place. They believed the advent of white men into our country was the cause of this change. They believed with a tenacity for which our race is noted, in the principles of their forefathers. They had been taught to believe the white man was their enemy, and they resented the intrusion of a civilization that would change all their established habits. They saw with jealous eyes how quickly the younger men grasped new ideas and customs; how readily the young women accepted the attentions of white men who came among them. But with characteristic optimism they put aside gloomy forebodings and spent many happy hours together in carefree intercourse.

Our people had little envy, if not entirely devoid of it, yet there was a kind of merry rivalry among the different social groups or branches of the Um-so-ma. The comradeship or partisanship existing between those of the same branch was outstanding, and it meant a delightful feeling of kinship or intimacy, a kind of fellowship which afforded much merriment and innocent fun among both old and young. There were many jokes, always directed against or at the expense of those who belonged to other branches of the Um-so-ma, though nothing sordid or vulgar ever entered into this fun. Always there was observed that simple courtesy and consideration which I have mentioned before, and which was the very foundation of all our social intercourse, yet lacking in those meaningless, foolish forms that have sham and hypocrisy for their foundation.

When two of our men went hunting together or happened to come together when hunting in the woods, the first game killed or trapped by either of them was graciously offered to the other, with the remark "Gi tap-il-wa-ha-la" which signifies "I enliven your spirit," or "Gita il-ani cha-la" which means "I enliven you as to a man."

The game thus presented always was courteously received, accepted with the remark "Ni-ya-wa" (I thank you), but the ordinary expression "Gi dap-hala" (I present you) was avoided in this case, as lacking in heartiness.

There was one invariable exception to this custom of giving the first game to a companion, and that was when an otter was killed. An otter was always retained by the man who had killed it, with congratulations from the other. If one presented an otter by mistake or by overcourtesy, it was indignantly refused, and the person who made such a mistake was gravely lectured by his elders.

I remember one time my father killed an otter when I was with him and others were present. I asked him why he did not *tap-ilwah-iwa* (enliven with it). He then explained that there were very serious reasons for this exception, but I cannot recall just what they were. It certainly was not because an otter was a rare animal and its fur very valuable, but because of some sentimental reason. "In honor preferring one another" was the code of one Shawnee to another, although the title of "gentleman" was unknown. Nor was there any pretense about it, just a natural, simple courtesy that existed, rather than was taught or exacted.

Hunting or trapping otters was one of the most fascinating sports we had in those days. In addition to the value of their skin, they were very rare and hard to catch, and even Indians were not free from the love of doing something unusual. I remember one hunting expedition that I went on with my father. With us were two friends of my father, Alex Marhardy and Jim Lighthorse. We camped on Deep Fork, a few miles east of the Sauk and Fox Agency. The stream was noted for its animal inhabitants, and in the evening we set traps for beaver, otter, and other fur-bearing animals, all along the stream for quite a distance. Near our camp was a pond, evidently the result of a recent overflow, about four or five feet deep. The next morning was very frosty, but quite early we went to look into our traps. Jim and Alex took their rifles, but father and I did not, so that we might be free to carry any game that we might find in the traps. They went along the west side of the pool, father and I had the east side.

Just as we all reached opposite positions on the pool we startled something which resulted in a terrible commotion in the water, as if huge fishes were chasing each other in the water. "*Kit-taw-tay*" (an otter), father cried and ordered me to run back to the camp for his gun. Away I ran, just as if life depended upon it, and soon returned with the gun. Both the other men had their guns ready to fire, and it became a contest, which would not have been allowed under any other circumstance. All three men stood, tense, searching with keen eyes for the ripple on the surface of the water that would show where a small black speck would appear, as the otter would push its nose slightly above the water to get air—its breath would cause the lively ripple. It always appeared near a drift or brush.

Father had a slight advantage, because the light of the rising sun was to his back, while it shone in the eyes of the other men on the west side. It was an exciting moment! Then father saw the tiny black spot, and his shot rang through the woods with loud echoes. The otter jumped high clear of the water, then tried to wriggle out to the bank, for it was only stunned by the shot. But father ran around the drift and finished it with a club. It was a huge otter, and Jim and Alex helped father carry it up the bank, all the while congratulating him on his success. My father's face reflected his happiness although he remained silent. It was my expecting him to do with this game as he would have done with any other, that caused me to ask the question: "Why did he not enliven our friends by giving them the otter?"

As our people had no almanacs or calendars, records of time were kept only in memory, and even to me it is a wonder how accurately they could calculate the passing of the seasons. Today, I cannot tell more accurately the season than could my father or mother reckoning by moons and the signs of nature. Thirteen moons made a year, and dates were kept by the fulling or waning of the moon. The position of the sun was watched closely. At dawn, at sunrise, when the sun was high in the heavens, when the sun hung low in the sky, at dusk, or at the setting of the sun—all were significant hours to be observed. There were certain stages of the moon to be observed in almost every work undertaken, and in this I have seen a similarity in superstitious persons of the white race. I know white people who will plant potatoes and some other seed only in certain stages of the moon, who will not make soap except before the moon reaches its full, believing the soap would shrink away. Our people believed that if clapboards were made for roofing their cabins after the moon reached its full the clapboards would curl up at their loose ends on the roof. Who can say how much of this is superstition and how much pure wisdom? I learned at an early age to observe closely all signs given us to judge by. To all who will listen and look, nature reveals most astounding secrets.

One of the most sacred rites of our people was called *Tak-u-wha Nag-a-way* (Bread Dance), and I am glad to say that the custom still is followed though not with the sincerity and faith that characterized the dances I remember in my youth. Our people believed that before they planted a crop or started the important work of the new year they should hold a Bread Dance when the Great Spirit would be implored to bless the people and give them a bounteous crop and a prosperous, peaceful year. Contrary to the white man's idea of religion—which seems to require a gloomy countenance when praying for a blessing—the Shawnees believed that in order to obtain a blessing they should show a merry spirit and a contented countenance. Therefore when we sought a blessing it required an occasion when all were gay and cheerful, and we looked forward to the spring Bread Dance, as to our most festive occasion. The Bread Dance really opened the festivities of spring and summer, when all nature seemed to be rejoicing and happy. Not until after this important ceremony would anyone venture to plant a crop of corn or undertake any important work.

The time for celebrating the Bread Dance was determined as follows: Early in the spring when the buds began to swell on the trees, the birds began to sing and chatter to their mates, the wild ducks and geese departed for their northern homes, the air became soft and warm, the sun rose earlier, the days grew longer. Reciting all these evidences of the passing of winter, the chief gave orders to his people to make preparations for their festival of the Bread Dance. *But even then the dance could not be held until after the full of the moon.*

CEREMONIALS AND SOCIAL LIFE

VIII

AS THE Bread Dance is considered a religious rite the
preparations for the dance and festival were under the
supervision of the chief of the *Pec-ku-we* clan who by virtue
of his clan had charge of all matters relating to our religion,
or to the Great Spirit. There are two standing committees,
one composed of twelve men, the other of twelve women,
who actually have charge of the arrangements. These committees are appointed by the chief of the *Pec-ku-we* clan for
life, or during good behavior. Each group has a leader who
is appointed by the chief. Two of my sisters, Nancy and
Nellie, are members of this committee today. Nancy, the
elder, is the leader of the women's committee.

Here again we see a great difference between the customs
of the white people and of our race, because generally only
the young white people dance, while the presence of the
very old members of our tribe is desired at our dances to lend
dignity and honor to the occasion, and they always take
part in the dance.

The committees are designated *nay-na-how-aych-ki* (preparation utterers), or *may-yaw-thech-ki* (those in line by birth).
When the proper time for the celebration arrives—it is
watched for and recognized by all the people—the chief
assembles both of the committees and makes his appointments to fill vacancies if any exists. He then informs them
that the time has arrived for them to perform their duties
to their people and to the Great Spirit. Very solemnly he

repeats to them the tradition connected with the festival, the dance and its proper observance. He sets a date for the twelve men to begin their hunt for the game required for the feasts. Only certain kinds of game should be used for this feast, namely deer, wild turkey, quail or grouse, and squirrel.[1]

After all the instructions are given to the committees the chief opens a ball game that is peculiar to this event, in which the men play against the women, and all the people who have assembled may take part if they so desire. The losing side must provide the wood for the fires at the Bread Dance. As the grounds are brilliantly lighted by bonfires at the time of the dance, which sometimes lasts two nights, the preparation of the wood is no small matter. The game is animated and lively, but whichever side loses undertakes the gathering of the wood cheerfully.

The twelve men begin at once to get ready for the hunt. They set out for three days, not forgetting to take along some of the parched meal which always is carried as an emergency ration. Those who are to get the wood make sure there is enough for cooking the game and to supply the big bonfires which illuminate the grounds for as many nights as the frolic is to continue. All the people gather at the dance ground and camp, waiting and ready for the return of the hunters. There is a ritualistic order in the arrangement of the tents that is followed scrupulously. Often there are visitors from other tribes, and there is much quiet visiting as old friends sit about the campfires and tell stories. The women are busy with the pots and kettles. The air is filled with the odor of cooking food. The dance ground is cleaned and marked off. Seats are placed at the west side of the

1. Since our state game laws forbid the killing of most of these game at the season when the Bread Dance is held, only squirrels are used for the meat at the Bread Dances. Special permission from the state game warden is required for the Indians to kill enough squirrels for the proper observance of this feast.

ground for the singers, logs are arranged along the other sides as seats for the crowd or those who tire of dancing.

On the third day the hunters return at sunrise. They approach the camp ground in single file, with an occasional whoop, and now and then a rifle shot. The singers take their places and begin to beat on their drums. All the people gather at the dance ground, standing outside the square. As the twelve hunters reach the dance ground they are met by the women's committee who take charge of the game, and prepare it for cooking. The men then pass into the dance ground square, still in single file, the leader at the head of the line. Four songs are sung by the singers, as they beat on their drums in a rhythmic monotonous strain. The men move in a circle, in slow, solemn, graceful movements. When four songs are sung the dance is ended for the time being, and a hearty breakfast is served to the twelve hunters. All conversation is in a subdued voice, as the people wait quietly for the next part of the dance. Even the children go about their play quietly.

Several hours pass before the game and a great quantity of bread prepared in several different ways is all done. It is all brought and laid on a clean white cloth in the center of the dance ground, and carefully covered over with another white cloth. The people then gather around the dance ground, and a prayer is offered by a man versed in the ancient customs and forms as handed down from generation to generation by word of mouth, from time immemorial. This man generally is an orator. He asks the Great Spirit for fruitfulness of the coming season; that the people may be given an abundant crop of corn and beans and pumpkins. He prays for the general welfare of the people, for success in all their undertakings, and voices an eloquent prayer for an increase in game. He then thanks the Great Spirit for the success of the hunters during the past winter, and for all the good things that have come to the people during their lives.

After this prayer or declamation—it usually is a wonderful piece of oratory—the serious side of the occasion is over, and the people begin the dance which is as follows: The women congregate in compact form in front of the singers who continue to sing as they beat a weird, rhythmic music on their tom-toms. The women sing with them, and move with a slight swaying motion of the body, right and left. A certain phrase in the song ridicules the weakness of human nature. This phrase when sung by the men is directed against the women, and when sung by the women is directed against the men (both men and women are singing). In spite of the reticence practiced, murmurings can be heard in the crowd which show their sympathy with the singers. The women exclaim "the women conquer," or the men cry out "the men have conquered," showing a pleasant, friendly rivalry between the sexes.

This is followed by the dance around the ring by the two committees. Twelve men dance inside the circle, and twelve women dance outside the circle of men, each line being led by an appointed leader. In this dance all the people may take part, but they must follow the committee, and under no circumstance must one break into, or enter the file. This dance continues at intervals with the slow musical rhythm of tom-toms until late in the afternoon, when all partake of the feast. The men of the committee distribute the bread, and the women the meat. There is no restraint upon their joyousness and good humor as they eat of the feast.

At dusk the frolic dance begins and is continued throughout the night; when men and women dance together, as they sometimes do, the formation is one behind the other. The music for this part of the dance is much faster and louder than for the sacred ceremonial dance following the prayer. The dance usually closes at sunrise, and each family goes home with a glorified feeling of having appeased the Great Spirit.

The dances that follow the Bread Dance, such as the Green Corn dance, are for frolic and fun. Each has its own set of songs and customs, but they are not considered obligatory. The Bread Dance was, and is, always observed strictly according to the accepted tribal custom.

In the olden times no corn was ever planted by the Shawnees until after the Bread Dance, and since the full of the moon sometimes appeared late, the corn accordingly was planted late, which often resulted in a short crop despite the eloquent prayer of the master of ceremonies at the dance.

In some dances frolic dances—the men and women join hands to form a circle, but not side by side, as white people do. A man holds his hand out behind him which is taken by a woman with a handkerchief or cloth in her hand. She in turn extends her other hand behind her, which is taken by another man. In this dance a young woman is permitted to select the brave she wishes to dance with, by simply taking her place behind him. When she extends her hand, if it is bare—not protected by the handkerchief—it is an indication that he will be acceptable to her as a lover or perhaps a husband. If he likes her looks or is impressed with her personality, he is at liberty to make further advances. But always there is a great reserve and little mention is made of affection, if indeed any at all. Yet I sincerely believe that there was just as much affection between men and women of our race in the olden times as there was in any other race. The Shawnee young people of today seem to have adopted the white man's way of courtship, as they have his way of marriage. I believe the young women rather like to be talked to about love, and are not so willing to take that emotion for granted.

Another sport that was enjoyed by our people was a ball game which was played early in the summer by both men and women. But after the month of June—as we counted the seasons—the ball season was closed with a pretty ceremony that put the ball away until the time for the Bread Dance the next spring. All these rules and ceremonies were known to all the people, and they were respected, observed, and kept sacred and inviolate.

About the middle of August the chief of the Kis-pu-go clan, who had charge of all matters relating to war, held a war dance. We called that *I-la-ni-wag-a-way* (man dance, or brave dance). In this dance the music was louder and more of a martial nature, when war whoops took the place of the softly crooned songs of the dance described above. This dance was somewhat official, but often was followed by other dances for frolic only, until the end of the season.

Early in the fall—about the middle of September by the calendar—the dance was held that closed the season for dances until the next spring. This was somewhat similar to the spring Bread Dance, except that it took the form of a thanksgiving ceremony, when a prayer of gratitude was offered to the Great Spirit, and an earnest petition for an abundant game season. During the winter there was much visiting together of the people, when the men went on hunting trips together, or would sit about the campfire and tell stories. It was at these times that the most lively jokes were told about one's Um-so-ma, when groups lined up and thought up things that would make their adversaries appear ridiculous. Those story-tellers were masters of the art. They could tell offhand a story that would contain suspense, mystery, and surprise, with never a change of countenance to betray the fact that it was fiction of the purest kind, until it might be accepted, swallowed whole, by those listening. Then the merriment that would follow!

.   .   .   .

I was nine years old when my mother died. She had been ailing for several days, and we children knew that there was something unusually wrong with her, but we were not allowed to go into the cabin where she lay. Father told us she was *ah-qui-lo-ky* (ill). Some of the neighbor women were with her, and a medicine man from Little River came to see her. A great sadness seemed to hover over the earth. It was only a few days, probably four or five, when I passed the door and saw that she was carefully covered with a white cloth, and all the women were silently weeping. Father came to where we children were sitting, gloomy and sad, and told us that our mother was *ah-san-wah* (vanished, or disappeared), an expression that always is applied to the death of a person by the Shawnees. A great many people came to the house. Everything was done in an orderly way and very quietly. There were no noisy protestations of grief, though sorrow was in every heart, for my mother was much loved by her people.

Just a little way from the house a grave was dug, and at the appointed time four men carried the body to the grave, by straps placed beneath it, and lowered it into the grave. Then a silent procession formed at the house, with my father at the head, we children next, then relatives and friends.

Between the house and the grave an elderly man stood with a small buckskin bag held open in his hand; it contained sacred tobacco, which always was used on such occasions. As the procession passed him, each person dipped his thumb and forefinger into the bag, taking a small bit of the tobacco, holding it thus, as he passed around the

[63]

grave, from the foot to the head; there he would stoop slightly as he dropped the tobacco into the grave.

The procession continued until all had passed by the open grave, and returned to the house. Last came the elderly man who had held the tobacco; he knelt at the head of the grave, and holding a bit of the sacred tobacco over the grave he made remarks. He called the deceased by name, and implored her not to allow the sorrow of her husband and children and other relatives to hinder her on her journey into that happy world beyond, but to go serenely and happily as was intended by *Kuh-koom-they-nah* (our Grandmother, or Great Spirit). Then after dropping a bit of the tobacco into the grave, he said it was true that her husband and children, her relatives and friends were full of sorrow, for that was *wa-chi-tah* (natural, or intended), but their sorrow soon would be wiped out by the goodness of Kuh-koom-they-nah. The love they had for her here should make her happier in the land to which she had gone, and still happier would be their meeting when they joined her in the next world. The man then finished dropping the tobacco into the grave, which was covered by the men who had carried the body.

Although outwardly we were calm, our hearts were torn with grief as deep and sincere as ever children felt for their parent. Some of our neighbors remained to cheer us. The women cleaned the cabin thoroughly, and swept the yard. These good friends stayed with us until the fourth day, when everyone bathed, even to our hair, and changed into fresh, clean clothes. Then a ceremony of cheer was held for father and for us, in which we were advised to lay aside our grief and be happy, for so our departed loved one would wish us to do.

This rite of cheer that followed the burial of my mother was used by the Shawnees for all deaths, only being a little different in the case where a widow was left with children by the death of her husband. Then it was as follows: For the first day after the burial of her husband a widow was allowed to give way to her grief; then she was advised to choose a man to take the place of the departed one, for the sake of her children. She should then rest herself with sleep, and take food for the ordeal before her. Then on the third day her friends gathered about her in the evening, and a cheerful night was passed. The men and women all assumed a lively manner, and told stories of the bravery of the men, interesting legends, and even jokes, to keep her interested. A preparation of herbs and cold water was wiped over her face at intervals, to keep her fresh and awake. As the sun began to rise, an elderly man, some relative or intimate friend, took a position at the back of the widow's seat and addressed her in this manner: "My daughter, your husband has vanished, and has left you alone with your little children. He was a good man [there follows a list of his good qualities], but he is gone. It is not right that you should grieve for him; he would not have it so. It is right that you should select some man to take his place and be a father to your little children."

He then called upon her to select the man whom she would like to take the place of her departed husband. If she selected one, the friends departed and left them alone together. This little ceremony of cheer was regarded as a marriage ceremony. If the widow did not select her mate, the usual order of selection was used, which simply was the desire expressed by two people to take up the duties of life together. No ceremony was then necessary.

The Shawnee Indians of fifty years ago, contrary to general belief, were a very sociable people. The greatest differences between their social life and that of the white people was the deference paid to old age by the Indians, and the association of the sexes. In all our gatherings and in our home life the older people "had the floor" so to speak. They were given consideration by the younger people, their counsel and advice listened to with respect. Young people were taught to guard their facial expressions and to control their passions so thoroughly that to do so became second nature; perhaps I might even leave off the "second." The higher the class of family, the greater the self-control of its members.

Consider, we had no newspapers to disseminate the doings of our people or the news of the world at large. There were no shows, no places of public amusement, but there was comparative leisure for the enjoyment of friends, because the simple life we lived did not demand a continual strife to provide the necessities for existence. Hence visiting was much enjoyed. There was little strain on hospitality, for a visitor usually contributed something to the larder of his host, and sleeping quarters meant simply a shelter from the elements. The men enjoyed hunting together. Parties would go out and hunt during the day, and sit about a campfire at night and talk. Natural history was a subject that always was interesting; traditions often told were embellished with the lively imagination of the speaker. Stories relative to one's Um-so-ma, or against the Um-so-ma of the others present was one phase of story-telling that gave vent to all the wit and humor of the narrator.

The Shawnee language is peculiar in that it contains few idioms, and does not lend itself to light and familiar speech; but it is effective in oratory and impressive with a stately manner. Our belief that all nature was animate, sympathetic, and responsive gave color to the speeches of orators and chiefs. When the warrior Tecumseh made his famous speech in behalf of the confederacy of the different tribes in Indiana his references to Mother Nature were considered merely poetical, but in reality they voiced the sincere belief of his people. On one occasion he cried, "the very trees of the forest drop tears of pity upon us as we walk beneath them," which illustrates the feeling of actual kinship with nature that existed in his mind.

When I was a child we had a distant relative May-gil-aw-fan-i who visited us occasionally. He was a good story-teller and when he was with us our neighbors would gather to hear him talk. We would all sit about the campfire and listen for hours. For him mother always prepared *O-sah-saw-po* (corn and nuts cooked together), which was his favorite dish.

There were no courtships among our young people such as there are today. Usually marriages were arranged by the parents. The parents of a son seeing a maiden they thought would make a fit wife for their son, would approach her parents with a proposal for their son. Either of the young people might object, in which case there was no compulsion, but as parents were usually more particular than young people, their wishes were considered in the matter. However, young people sometimes did arrange matters for themselves. For instance, should a maiden like the looks or the manner of a young brave she might seek a place behind him in the dance, as I have mentioned before, and give him her hand without a handkerchief. The giving of the naked hand always denoted a "willingness" to be regarded as a future mate. Then the young man could, if he desired, make further advances. This he did in a very dignified way. There were no gushing speeches, no promises, but a perfect understanding resulted from the few words quietly spoken, the glances of affection, and perhaps a handclasp.

Having arrived at such an understanding the two announced their intentions to their respective families, and took up their lives together, and built a we-gi-wa or cabin for their home. Usually there was a period of feasting, each family contributing to the good cheer, and all the intimate friends enjoying the occasion. There was no marriage ceremony, neither were there any divorce courts. Once in a great while a man would desert his wife, but it was not regarded as the proper thing to do, and with us public opinion or the opinion of our friends made our social laws.

We had no positive laws forbidding polygamy, but it was very seldom practiced, and was frowned upon by our people with just as much condemnation as would the white people of today resent the intrusion of such a social error, considered from a social standpoint alone. Our laws did not forbid a man having two wives, but our social system did not approve of such a situation, hence it was avoided. An Indian cannot endure being ostracized by his people.

It may be interesting to note here that when the Indian Territory was opened for white settlement and old tribal laws gave way to state and United States statutes, there was found only one man among the Shawnee tribe who had two wives.

HARD TIMES AND PROSPERITY

IX

I REMEMBER very little that took place during the next few months after my mother died. Our family life must have been terribly broken up, but as usual, I followed my father about and spent very little time about the home place. My older sister Nancy took up the burden of caring for our home and for the younger children. In this she was assisted by the women of the neighborhood, who never were too busy with their own affairs to help one in need. They would have divided their last morsel of food with us, and possibly did do so at times.

Father went about hunting and fishing as usual, and in due time he planted a crop, with the help we boys gave him. His health must have improved a great deal; I do not remember him having an attack of his disease during that first year after mother left us.

Mother had been dead about a year when father took another wife. This was a very simple matter, as I have already set forth: just a decision of two people to take up life together, and in this particular case the woman must adopt father's children as her own. This was just as binding as the religious or legal ceremony of other people.

The woman father selected for his wife was perhaps thirty years old and had never been the wife of another man. She was a strong, capable, industrious woman. She came into our home and assumed the care and responsibility of the family cheerfully; she was always kind to the children and to father, and we all became deeply attached to her. After a time our family life went on practically the same as it had done before mother's death.

It was the year that mother died that an influx of Citizen Pottawatomie Indians occurred. The treaty that had been made with the Shawnees immediately after the Civil War which gave them authority to return to this section of the Indian Territory had never been ratified, thus the records did not show that this land had been assigned to any tribe. When the state of Kansas wanted the land then occupied by the Pottawatomie Indians for its white settlers the government persuaded the Indians to come to the Indian Territory and promised them thirty square miles of land which it had acquired from the Seminoles between the North Fork of the Canadian and the Canadian rivers. But they were told to take land not claimed by any other tribe. The Shawnees already had settled and occupied the land included in this territory, mostly the north half of it. When the Pottawatomies came into the country there was a great deal of unpleasantness, hard feelings, and nearly a war between the two tribes. The Pottawatomies claimed the whole tract, and insisted upon settling among the Shawnees. They would select a homesite and erect a cabin, then some of our people would go by night or when the family was away from home, and tear it down. Sometimes there would almost be a fight. This went on for some time, then the government took a hand, and would put the Shawnees off the land, but a delegation of Friends went to Washington and presented the matter to the President, who interfered, and the matter was settled temporarily. But there was much discontent and idleness and worry over the situation among the Shawnees. The addition of many hunters in the woods made game scarce, and little farming was done because of the unsettled condition. At times there was real distress because of the scarcity of food. This went on for several years.

I remember a time when there was an unusually hard year. A drouth had cut short the crop of corn, and game was very scarce. Actual want stared us in the face. My father with a party of other men started out to find a place where there was game or where food was more plentiful. We tramped for several days, then camped near where the city of Sapulpa now stands. But there seemed to be no game in the woods. The men became very discouraged and gloom settled over the company as they gave way to superstitious fear. Surely the Great Spirit had deserted them! Perhaps there was something wrong with their families at home! Afraid of no living man, impervious to any form of physical suffering, these men became weak and inefficient hunters at the thought of harm coming to their homes.

One day my father was feeling so bad that he could not go with the other men when they went out to hunt, and I of course stayed with him. We actually were hungry. The men had been gone several hours when I heard a terrible sound coming through the woods. It sounded to me like a child screaming in pain. On it came, closer and closer, until suddenly we saw a great wildcat come tearing through the brush. Father was unable to stand, but he raised on his elbow, and took aim at the cat as it vanished into the brush, and fired. The shot took effect in the cat's head and it fell over dead.

I hastily skinned the cat, which was a huge one, but young and tender, and fat as a pig. I put it to barbecue on a stick, and when the men came back tired, hungry, and discouraged, we had a satisfying meal—of wildcat. Its fur was valuable too, being unusually fine. I remember that the party went home the next day, but I do not remember how we managed to get food during that long winter.

One peculiar incident illustrates a freak of nature that I never have heard anyone else mention. It happened early one morning when father and I went out on a hunting expedition. We were sitting very quietly near the edge of a high bluff overlooking the Canadian River, waiting for game to appear. The position gave us a good view of a large area of country. Suddenly we heard a peculiar sound, as if it were the rustling of dead leaves by some creature, but we were unable to locate the direction from which the noise came. We moved cautiously towards the edge of the bluff, and there we saw a strange sight! A huge rattlesnake was moving slowly, with dried leaves protruding from every scale. It went slowly towards a ledge of rock and disappeared from sight with its load of leaves under a ledge within twenty feet of where we watched. Father thought the rattler, whose scales could be opened at will, managed to catch the leaves in its scales and used this method to carry them into the rocks for its winter bed. It evidently opened its scales in the pile of leaves, caught leaves under the scales, then drew them close to its body, holding the leaves. Later the rattler came backing out from the rocks and disappeared in the bed of leaves.

When I was in school in the East I told of this experience in class when we were discussing natural history, and our teacher expressed the opinion that the rattler did not build its nest for warmth, for it was a cold-blooded creature, but prepared a bed in which to hide, as a protection from other creatures during its long winter sleep.

There must have been a migration of game back into our country, for I do not remember another year that was so hard as the one I have mentioned. Besides game, we had plenty of nuts too, pecans, walnuts, and some hickory nuts, wild fruits, and occasionally wild honey. The apple trees that father set out bore good fruit, and altogether I think we had a long spell of prosperity. Also, our people must have been more industrious, for there was plenty of good food in our homes.

But there was a feeling of uncertainty and uneasiness everywhere, because the trouble with the Pottawatomies had not been settled. There was talk of allotting the land, and the Shawnees asked that they be given two hundred acres per capita. This was denied them, and on May 23, 1872, an Act of Congress was passed whereby allotments were made to both the Pottawatomies and the Shawnees. The quantity of land allotted to the Pottawatomies was just double that allotted to the Shawnees. This resulted in more trouble to the government, and ill will between the tribes. Some time during the year 1872 our principal chief John White died, and this added to the unsettled feeling. He had been one of our most powerful and wise leaders, and the people trusted him and depended upon him for guidance. After his death John Sparney became principal chief, Uncle Joe Ellis remained second chief, and my uncle Big Jim was chief of the Pec-ku-we clan. There were many meetings of the council, and much grave discussion around the camp-fires.

There was a feeling among our people that some of our young men should be educated so that they could read and write, and understand what was written in the treaties and old documents in our possession. Some thought we would be more able to take our own part in controversies that were continually arising between our people and the government, if our young men could read. Or, as one chief put it, "it would enable us to use the club of white man's wisdom against him in defense of our customs and our Mee-saw-mi as given us by the Great Spirit."

The Society of Friends of Philadelphia had sent missionaries to visit among our people occasionally. We trusted them fully, and they advised the chiefs to educate all their young people. There was much discussion on the subject; education meant civilization, white man's ways, and change, to the people, and they wanted only to be left to themselves. But finally the missionaries decided to open a school in connection with a mission they had planned to open for the Shawnee Indians. The site selected for the mission was about a mile and a half from the Canadian River on a splendidly wooded hill, overlooking the country for miles and miles in every direction.

THE MISSION SCHOOL

X

THE mission was built about one-third of a mile from my father's cabin. He was one of the few Indians of that time who really believed in education, and he heartily endorsed the efforts of the Friends. In fact he helped to haul the lumber used in the building from the Sauk and Fox Agency, about thirty miles distant as the crow flies, but much farther by wagon roads. There was a government saw mill at the Agency, and the lumber was donated for the new school and church building.

I remember an incident that happened while the mission was being built that had a marked effect on my life. One damp, foggy morning while we were eating breakfast a white man came to our door. He told father he was one of the men working on the new mission building. He had come out to look for some mules that had strayed away from the place during the night, and had gotten lost in the fog. Having forgotten his compass, he was unable to find his way back.

Father had acquired some understanding of English during his service in the army, and he invited the stranger to eat breakfast, which invitation was gladly accepted. After the man had eaten heartily, father led him back through the woods to the place where he had been working. His manner was very different from what we had been taught to expect from white men, for he was full of smiles and kindness as he talked with father while eating his breakfast. He spoke kindly to us children too. His name was Thomas H. Stanley, and he was the traveling Friend missionary.

When the mission was finished, and a day school opened, six Indian children and I were admitted, and were given English names. This man remembered his visit to our cabin and suggested that I be given his name, Thomas. In the years that followed I learned to know him quite well, and I owe much to his kindness toward me. In fact Thomas H. Stanley was very kind to all our people, being always sympathetic and patient, ready with sound advice not only on spiritual matters, but on our daily problems, down to the adjustment of our farming implements.

The mission when first opened consisted of one building about fourteen by twenty-eight feet, divided into two rooms. The missionary, Joseph Newsom, and his family lived in one room, and the other was used for the schoolroom and office. The furniture was crude, but seemed wonderful to Indian children.

When I entered the school I was twelve years old, and could speak no word of English, except the word "soldier" which was my nickname. I no longer had any fear of white people, but had a great desire to learn their ways. In fact for a long time there had been a question in my heart for which I could find no answer. I loved my people and I liked their ways; I had a profound respect for and confidence in those men who were my father's friends, who had such a bitter hatred against the white race, or rather against those things which the white race represented. There were some warm friendships between Indians and white men, but generally the Indians hated the thought of civilization. Deep down in my nature however, there was a yearning desire for things which civilization represented. I hardly knew what it was that I desired, young as I was, yet I was conscious of a deep and unsatisfied longing. Something, some inner voice, told me there was a better life, a better way of living than my people knew.

Thus it was that when my sister Nancy and I started to the mission school, I was eager to learn all that was taught me. But I had been so drilled and instructed in the art of concealing my feelings that I, like the other Indian children, presented an appearance of utter indifference.

In warm weather the boys wore one garment, simply a long shirt usually made of calico that our fathers bought from the licensed traders. In winter we added leggings to this dress, and sometimes a hunting shirt was worn over the calico one. The hunting shirt was made of tanned buckskin, fringed all around the bottom, the collar, the sleeves, and the pocket. We wore shoes or boots when we could get them, but generally we went barefoot. We had no hats, but sometimes wore caps made of the skin of a wildcat, a coon, or a beaver, with bunches of feathers puffed or stripped from the stem to look like a fine plume, placed on the top of the cap. We boys wore our hair short, very much as the girls of today wear their hair bobbed. This is the way Shawnee men always have worn their hair. Never did they braid it, as some other tribes do.

The girls however, wore their hair long and braided. Sometimes they wore a colored handkerchief tied about their heads; more often they went bareheaded. They wore long dresses of calico or linsey, a coarse half wool material, with skirts gathered full about the waist. After the school was established our good friends of the East sent us through our missionary some clothing like white children wore, usually discarded clothing their own children had worn. They even sent clothes for the women and men occasionally, which delighted them as much as it did the children. We took our lunch and stayed from early morning until about

[77]

four o'clock in the afternoon. Some of the children had to walk more than four miles to school.

I do not remember what books we studied at first. Our teaching must have been mostly oral. We wanted to learn words that white children used in their play. We quickly learned words that were commonly used, such as game, deer, cat, dog, duck, bow, and arrow. After we had learned to spell and read, we used McGuffey's readers, and they opened to us many wonderful visions of the life of white people, especially white children.

In that school we learned to read and to write, to spell and to cipher, and we were also taught a new idea of serving the Great Spirit—the personal way white people served Him. We also learned a new sense of the fitness of things, such as expressing gratitude with the words "thank you," when receiving, and the word "please," when asking for anything. We learned to be neater in our personal habits, to wash ourselves oftener, to comb our hair properly, to keep our clothing cleaner. We learned the rudiments of courtesy, such as to open a door for a woman, to enter a room with our heads bared, and to express in our manner those principles which I have stated before were the mainsprings of all our intercourse—consideration for others.

I remember a clash of wills that I had with one of my teachers, Miss Ella D. Coltrane, after I had been in school about a year. Someone gave me some paints, red, blue, and green. With laborious care I painted my face in what I thought to be a fine example of Indian art, and went to school.

When school opened Miss Coltrane came and sat by me and looked at me intently. I began to feel embarrassed. Presently Miss Coltrane said, "Tommy, did you try to draw a map on your face?"

I was terribly insulted, and rising abruptly, I hurriedly left the school and went home. But after a few days my desire for knowledge overcame my indignation, and I sheepishly returned to school. The teacher very wisely refrained from mentioning the incident or the cause of my absence from school, and things went on as before.

For two years the Friends held the day school in connection with the mission, then the government assumed control, added a new building and turned it into a boarding school. The Friends still exercised an influence in the management of the school, and conducted religious services in connection with the school. These good people who came among us and labored so patiently with us, were Friends in deed, as well as in name. While teaching us the ways of civilization and to read and write, they also set us an example of honesty and uprightness that did much to strengthen our faith in their lessons.

After the coming of the missionaries other white people often were seen. Several licensed traders opened stores at nearby points; their stores were filled with goods the Indians needed and were learning to regard as necessities.

Although the opening of the mission had meant a great deal to our people, government control of the school meant a great deal more. The Shawnees began to realize that civilization would be forced upon them as it had been on so many tribes in the East, and the more progressive ones accepted the fact. There was no way to evade it, so the best thing they could see to do was to get ready for it—to meet it. They sent their children to school so they might learn to fight the white men with his own weapons—words.

The Shawnees, as well as the Pottawatomies, Kickapoos, and Iowas, were under the jurisdiction of the Sauk and Fox Agency. After the government took over the mission school, it too was under the care of the Agency, and there was much more intercourse between the white people who lived about the Agency and our school. This helped the work of the teachers and gave them more congenial surroundings. More Indian children were sent to the school, and another teacher was added to the force. As the pupils advanced, the course of study was enlarged and became more interesting.

I attended the mission school two years, then went to the government school two years, and I learned rapidly. In fact I believe it is a compliment to the old methods of teaching when we consider the advancement a student could make in so short a time. At the end of those four years of school I could read and write reasonably well; I had mastered the first four rules of arithmetic to the complete satisfaction of my teachers, and I had a smattering knowledge of geography, physiology, grammar, and had taken a peep into the fascinating study of natural philosophy and other branches of higher learning and science. And I learned what was far more important—that I had only glimpsed the wonders of education. I had only tasted the joy of knowing things, and I had a consuming thirst for more knowledge.

But while I and a few other young people had been learning the way of the white man and enjoying the knowledge gained, some of the older members of our tribe had been bickering and fretting over injustices that had been heaped upon them (as they considered the acts of the government). The Act of Congress that had allowed the allotting of land to the Pottawatomies and the Shawnees, giving the Pottawatomies just double the amount allowed the Shawnees, had caused so much unpleasant feeling and unhappiness that the very existence of the tribal government was threatened. Some of our people had learned that the best policy was to accept what the government saw fit to give them, and go their own way, doing the best they could with what they had. Others bitterly opposed this code and preferred to reject all propositions made them by the government. There was constant bickering and much friction.

In 1875 there was a division among the tribe, when those under the leadership of chiefs John Sparney and Joe Ellis— called the progressives—accepted the allotments allowed by the government under the Act of Congress of May 23, 1872. Those under chiefs Big Jim and Sam Warrior, numbering nearly half the tribe—known to the government as the non-progressives—refused to accept the allotments. After much unhappiness among members of the tribe the non-progressives removed early in the spring of 1876 into the Kickapoo Reservation (which had not been allotted in severalty), north of the present town of Harrah, Oklahoma. There they resided for ten years, until they were removed by military force back to their own reservation in 1886.

Chief Big Jim and his councilmen John Welch and Pecan submitted a memorial to the Commissioner of Indian Affairs, in which they recited their reasons for leaving their reservation and asked assistance on account of their losses caused by moving, which claim finally was allowed.

HELPING TO EARN A LIVING—AMBITIONS

XI

DUE to my father's ill health I had to quit school in 1876 and help him make a living for the family. Since his second marriage several children had been born, Thompson B., Aleric, Casper, and James; all except the last named are among the living today.

Our needs had multiplied, and even then living expenses had begun to mount. Our people no longer were satisfied with the meager necessities of existence, that formerly had seemed sufficient. With the advent of traders' stores there were so many things to tempt one to buy, and with the bit of civilization we had learned there was a greater inclination to buy. It seemed that civilization was nothing more or less than a multiplication of man's needs and wants. There was an ever increasing demand for money—a commodity that only a few years before had not seemed a necessity.

As the people in the country increased in number, the game and wild animals decreased, while the price of pelts and furs was the same as before, or perhaps lower. We hunted and trapped and fished industriously when not engaged in working our crops, but the supply always was less than the need.

Most of my father's land was rich valley soil, but only about ten acres were cleared for cultivation, and our farming methods were crude indeed. The only implement we possessed for breaking the soil and cultivating the crops was a plow, cast whole into one piece, which made a furrow about ten inches wide. It had wooden beams and handles. We hitched one horse to it, by means of a single-tree and chains. It took four rounds of this plow to cultivate between rows. The first round was made close to the row of corn, turning the soil away from the corn; the second was made in returning, close to the opposite row, throwing the soil away, as before, which formed a ridge between the rows. The third round turned the soil back towards the corn, and by the fourth round the soil remaining in the ridge was thrown back towards the first row of corn. By this method it easily may be seen how long it would take to cultivate a field of corn. It may also be seen that we had no surplus corn to sell, even if we had had a market, which we did not have then.

My ambition while in school had been to prepare myself for the position of government interpreter. This position then was held by Robert Deer, who received one hundred dollars a year for his services, and that seemed like a great deal of money to me. When I had to give up school I feared that I never would be able to prepare myself for such a position, and I was deeply disappointed. But my father's will always had been my law, and I cheerfully set about helping him with the support of the family.

But only a short time elapsed before I was offered a position as interpreter by W. L. Austin who was the manager of a store owned by Nero Jones, a licensed trader at a post near the mission. While my use of English was somewhat limited then, I was able to interpret all that was necessary in this position. This post however, was soon abolished, and a new one established by Blossom and Clay, also licensed traders.

The new post was called Shawnee Town, and a post office was established, which shows that a good many white people had come into the country. I was employed by Blossom and Clay as interpreter, and later they hired me to look after their cattle as they grazed on the surrounding prairie.

These traders were good men, whose hearts were filled with kindness towards the Indians, and they did not strive to take advantage of our ignorance, as so many other traders had done. I believe if the Shawnees had had such traders among them in the early days there would not have been so much ill feeling and distrust of the white men, and the Indians would not have tried so hard to instill hatred and distrust in the hearts of their children.

During the time I worked for these men I learned a great deal about the ways of the white man and about civilization. Mr. Austin especially talked to me about the East, and a city called St. Louis. He told me that he would gladly help me to go to school, and even proposed that I should go with him when he returned to St. Louis and help him run a cigar store there. He said I could do that and go to school too. This idea was very pleasing to me, but when he went back to his home in St. Louis I could not leave my father, whose health failed steadily. He needed all the help I could give him in supporting the family.

Mr. Clay and Mr. Blossom were very kind to me. Mr. Blossom especially tried to encourage me in the pursuit of an education. He possessed more affability and probably was better educated than Mr. Clay, who was a man of few words. However, it is useless for me to extol the good qualities of these men, for they were well known to the early settlers of the country after it became Oklahoma Territory. When they gave up their trading post, Mr. Blossom went to Atoka, Indian Territory, where he owned a store and was postmaster for many years. He took a prominent part in the early development of that community. Mr. Clay went to Oklahoma City at the time of the opening of that part of

Oklahoma and went into business there. Later, when this country was opened for settlement he came back to our county seat. He married a Miss Biggs, and for several years they took a prominent part in the social life of the community, and accumulated considerable property. He and his wife moved to California where he died a few years ago. Both of these men left the impress of their characters on mine, for youth is impressed easily. My association with them continued, with some interruptions, for several years.

Although I had learned to read and write while in school, and had developed a great taste for reading, it was almost impossible to get books to read. Very few newspapers came into the country, and I suppose they were worn out from so much reading by white people. Very few people owned books of any kind; there were none to borrow, and none were offered for sale. Mr. Blossom, seeing my hunger for reading matter, suggested to me that I subscribe for *The Youth's Companion*, a weekly magazine published in Boston. At first it was hard for me to read it, for there were so many words and expressions used that I could not understand. I knew absolutely nothing of life as it was depicted in the stories, but I always was keenly interested in the pictures, and gradually I learned to understand the stories. I learned not only a better use of English, but a better knowledge of the conditions of life and the ways of the world. I remained a subscriber to this paper for many years.

While I had been in school I attended the mission services on Sundays, but after I went to work I was not able to do this regularly. Occasionally I did manage to go to church, and sometimes I visited with my friends, the teachers in the school. But most of my time was spent with the trader's cattle which needed grass on the Sabbath as well as on other days. Those long days that I spent with the cattle, riding my pony back and forth to keep them within their own grazing ground, sometimes sitting idly for hours on guard, while the cattle grazed peacefully, were days of deep thought. I pondered in my mind the things I had been told, and had read about civilization, and daily the conviction grew upon me that there was a better way to live than my people knew. All my visits with the teachers, my talks with the missionaries, fired my ambition and strengthened my determination to make something of myself. I had a keen desire to see other parts of the country which I read about, and things I saw in the pictures in my precious paper, but above all I wished to see the wonders of a large city.

PLANNING FOR AN EDUCATION

XII

ALL of my plans were thrown into confusion by the un-
expected death of my father, which occurred in the
summer of 1877. He was buried near our cabin with the
usual ceremony befitting his standing in the tribe.

Shortly before father's death my oldest sister Nancy had
married a man named William Charley who lived about
four miles east of us. After father's death our stepmother
contracted another marriage with a Shawnee named Elephant. She of course went with her children to live in his
house, and suddenly I found myself free to make such plans
and to undertake such things as I pleased about my future.
However I was under the guardianship of my uncle, my
mother's brother, Chief Big Jim, the non-progressive leader
of half of the tribe, and I felt that I should obey his wishes
in all things.

Family ties are binding in our tribe, and succession is
through the female line, therefore my uncle felt almost as
great a responsibility for me as if I had been his own son.
But he was the least progressive of our clan, and quite opposite to my father in all his views. Needless to say he had
little sympathy with my ambitions. For a time I felt very
much discouraged.

But the missionaries who had urged the Indians to send
their children to school often discussed education with the
chiefs and advised them to send some of their young men

East to be educated. The chiefs realized that times were changing, that the government was continually adopting new policies with the Indians, and that a tribe should have some of their men educated so that they might understand the treaties and messages sent from Washington. These things were discussed at all the councils, and whenever the missionaries and Indians talked together. The chiefs finally decided to send two young men East to be educated. They were to be selected from the two principal clans, the Tha-we-gi-la and the Pec-ku-we. The Tha-we-gi-la clan selected a young man named John King to represent them, and the Pec-ku-we clan decided to send me. At last my opportunity had come!

John King and I always had been very good friends, although we belonged to different clans. We were delighted that we were to go to school together and that together we would see the wonders of the world we had each heard so much about. John was eight years older than I, already a full grown man, and a good one. He had more experience than I in many things, but had attended school only a few months. Both of us were ambitious, and hoped to lead a life that would be worthwhile, though we differed in our philosophy. He longed for success in a business way, while I thought more about the mystery of life, the development of my mind, and the welfare of our people.

Many of the older settlers of the state will remember John King, for after his return from school he became a very successful merchant. First he had a store at old Shawnee Town, then one at Tecumseh, then the county seat, and later at Dale, near which town he held his allotment, and where he died, in 1901. He was prominent in the affairs of the Shawnee tribe and in the community in which he lived. He was progressive and had a good influence with the Indians and had many friends among the white people.

Well, John King and I had the consent of our chiefs to go away to school, but how were we to go? It took money to live in a civilized world, and schooling was not altogether free to us. There was no scholarship fund in the Shawnee tribe, as there was in many others. Most of our people were poor, and there was little money in the country.

Our good missionary Elkana Beard took the matter up with the Philadelphia Society of Friends who arranged for two scholarships for Indian boys in the Hampton Institute, at Hampton, Virginia. One was given by Miss Alice Longfellow in memory of her father, Henry Wadsworth Longfellow, and his appreciation of the Indian character. This scholarship was secured for me; the other was donated by another friend of the Indians, and was awarded to John King.

Hampton Institute was a normal training and agricultural school offering splendid opportunities to pupils who must work part time in order to pay expenses. It was coeducational and semi-military. The missionaries assured us that we would be able partially to support ourselves while attending school. With this hope of going to school in our hearts we saved our money carefully for months, so when the final arrangements were made and we were notified that the scholarships had been arranged, we had saved enough money to help us on our journey and to pay such entrance fees as would be required. How happy we were and how eager to begin our journey!

Just two days before we were to start for the East, two chiefs, my uncle Big Jim and Joe Ellis paid us a visit. They came just at dusk, in the evening, silently, in single file, from the west. Their manner of approach and their solemn faces told us very plainly that they had come in an official capacity, to convey to us instructions from the tribe. Their calm, dignified manner was ominous. When it was quite dark they called us to a caucus under the spreading branches of a great oak tree. We all squatted on the ground, in true Indian fashion.

Very solemnly the chiefs spoke to us. They reminded us of the responsibility we had assumed for our people when we consented to undertake the mission. We were not to go as individuals, but as representatives of the Shawnee tribe. The honor, the dignity, and the integrity of the tribe was placed in our hands. They told us of their desire that we should learn the white man's wisdom. How to read in books, how to understand all that was written or spoken to and about our people and the government. We should learn all this in order that when we came back we would be able to direct the affairs of our tribe and to assume the duties and position of chiefs at the death of the present chiefs. (Very well they knew that was our greatest ambition.) They pledged their words that we should be made chiefs of our respective clans. But there was a proviso attached to the promise that we would be chiefs—*a positive demand that we should not accept the white man's religion; we must remain true to the Shawnee faith.* If we did accept the new teachings, we would forfeit all hope of becoming chiefs. Fired with ambition and not realizing the importance of the obligation nor what it might mean to us, we solemnly pledged ourselves to remain true to the faith of our fathers.

The caucus lasted most of the night. The two chiefs were great men and wise ones in the principles and traditions of our tribe, and they talked to us of the life that was before us, its dangers and possibilities. They realized that we were young and that there would be a great many things that would be interesting to us, that might tempt us to forget the object of our sojourn in the land of the white men. But we must remain strong, take every advantage that was offered us to learn, but keep cool heads and hold council

[90]

with no one. Full well those men sensed that a crisis was near in the life of the Indian race, and that a change of some kind was inevitable. They wanted their people to be prepared for it, to understand all that was told to them. After listening to their grave counsel throughout the night, we felt very keenly the solemn obligation placed upon us, and assured them that we would remember their instructions.

Notwithstanding it had been the will of the chiefs that John King should go away to school, his family failed to see the honor that was being conferred upon him, and bitterly opposed his going. His older brother threatened to pursue him if he started, and force him to return. This did not weaken John's determination to go, but it forced us to conceal our plans and to make our preparations in secret. His family heard nothing of our going and no doubt decided that we had abandoned the idea.

But we had not been idle. From the chiefs who had made trips to Washington, and from everyone else who traveled, who had visited towns and cities, or who had ridden on trains we asked for information. And we received advice from them all. Some counseled us how to act when with strange people, how to get on trains, how to buy our food, how to conduct ourselves after our arrival. The missionaries too gave us advice, good advice. In fact we were so burdened with advice that we were more frightened than helped. Yet we were eager for the great adventure.

When the time came for us to start the missionary gave us a paper on which was written in a bold hand: "To whom it may concern." The paper told who we were, our destination, and for what purpose we were going to Hampton, Virginia. We were told to show this paper to conductors on the trains and to policemen. We were to know the conductors by the word "Conductor" on their caps, and the policemen by their blue uniforms, the club that they carried, or the star on their coats. In case we needed any advice we were to seek it from one of these men. It was the business of conductors to tell us what to do, and policemen always were to be trusted. We were instructed, needlessly, to be very careful to whom we talked, and under no conditions or circumstances were we to show our money to strangers. We secretly arranged with Elephant, the husband of my step-mother, to take us to Muskogee, that being the nearest rail-road point, about one hundred twenty miles distant.

Two Shawnee Councillors

Wah Pe Le The Indian Ter.
2d mo 15th 1876

Emma Kinson My Dear friend
Krecieved your letter about three
day ago. I will go to catch fish
some day. Pretty near time to
plant corn now. And pretty
near time to catch. But I got
no line though. But I got some
hooks, two of them, one little
and the other big one.
I like want to go in Indiana.
I want see cars, rail-roads
and other things.
its all I can say
Thy friend, I write again.

      Thomas Wildcat

THOMAS WILDCAT ALFORD'S FIRST LETTER

AN INDIAN CABIN OF YESTERDAY

A GROUP OF INDIAN FARMERS

GENERAL ARMSTRONG
PRINCIPAL OF HAMPTON INSTITUTE

THE YOUNG HAMPTON STUDENT
THOMAS WILDCAT ALFORD

SHAWNEE STUDENTS, 1887

BIRD'S NEST, HOME OF THOMAS WILDCAT ALFORD

CAMPUS OF OLD SHAWNEE SCHOOL SHOWING BUILDINGS ERECTED BY THACKERY

THE LITTLE MISSION CHURCH

EASTWARD HO!

XIII

IT WAS early in October, 1879, that John King and I set out for Hampton, Virginia. We left in the stillness of night, to avoid pursuit by John's family. We traveled all night and the next day, stopping only long enough for the mules to eat. We learned afterward that the threat of pursuit was not carried out, but we took no chances when we left.

In due time we arrived at Muskogee, now a thriving little city, but at that time a mere village. (But it looked very big to us then.) Happily we met there a man we had known at Shawnee Town; his name was Doctor Crane, and glad indeed were we to see a familiar face. He helped us when we went to buy our tickets and explained many things to us about the trip. When the marvelous passenger train came, with its shrieking engine and grating noises, Dr. Crane approached the conductor with us, to whom we showed our paper.

The conductor read the paper, looked us over, and motioned to us to enter the train. We said "goodbye" to Dr. Crane and entered the first passenger train we had ever seen. The sheer marvel of that coach! Can you imagine what those softly cushioned seats meant to us? Those carpeted aisles? The strange people who stared at us so intently?

The train began to move! We were on our way! Wonderful! Wonderful! But soon our worries began. There were many men and women on the train that day, and no doubt they meant to be kind to us. Several tried to show their interest by asking questions, trying to fit their words to what they conceived to be an Indian's understanding. But we were distrustful of them. We had never seen as many white people in our whole lives as were on the train that day. They looked very strange to us, and no doubt we looked queer to them, but we much preferred that they would leave us alone.

Although we had traveled all the night before and were very tired, there were too many interesting things to be seen for us to think of going to sleep. Besides we were afraid to go to sleep, for fear someone would take advantage of our unconscious state and rob us, or do us some bodily harm. Imagine a couple of white boys among as many Indians as there were white people on the train that day. Would they have thought of sleeping? But after a few hours, when we had become accustomed to the wonders we saw and were lulled and soothed by the motion of the train, we could hardly resist sleep, so we slept, one at a time. I sat vigilant and alert while John snatched a nap, then he would watch while I slept. We felt perfect confidence in the conductor, however, and did just what he told us to do.

Trains were not so fast then as now by a great deal, but in due time we arrived in St. Louis. The conductor led us to a large room in an immense building. There were a great many people there, and much noise and confusion. The conductor told us to sit down and wait, then he left us. We watched the people about us with interest, but we kept our faces free of any expression of curiosity. Some people were eating lunches, some were reading quietly, as if too accustomed to the sights to be seen on every hand to notice them. There was a lunch counter in the building, and we

[94]

bought a lunch. I remember that we each paid seventy-five cents for a half of a chicken to take with us, to eat on the train.

How long we waited there I do not know, but it seemed a long time to us. We could not understand the delay. Why didn't our train go on? Doctor Crane, whom we trusted fully, had told us that our tickets were "clear through." Every time a policeman came near us we produced our wonderful paper, but after reading it he would motion us to sit down and wait. While we waited, and before we had left the train we heard many remarks made about us, for as we spoke no English, evidently the people thought we could not understand what they said about us. This gave us a great deal of amusement, but we gave no sign that we understood or even heard these remarks. After a long time another conductor appeared, and we showed him our paper, which he read slowly, then showed us to his train. Once more we had a leader, and were on our way.

I recollect the impression made on my mind as we traveled over the beautiful country, through well cultivated fields, past beautiful homes, and through busy, bustling cities, and small towns. All was so strange to our eyes accustomed only to the western prairies and lowlands, or rolling timber lined hills. The deep, swift rivers, the beautiful mountain scenery, awe inspiring, marvelous. A wonderland indeed!

We had been told that when we reached a place called Baltimore we would leave the train and take a boat for the rest of the journey. When we arrived at Baltimore it was night. Evidently our train was late, for the conductor seemed concerned as he looked at his watch, and said "maybe-so boat gone." He then asked us how much money we had, but we became suspicious and would not tell him the exact amount, but gave him to understand that we had sufficient for our needs. He then called a man who was driving a closed carriage and ordered him to take us some place, which we did not understand, but we got into the carriage, and again our agony began. The driver turned first one way, then another. Into a broad, well lighted street, then into a narrow, dark one. We soon lost our sense of direction and could not tell whether we were going east or west, north or south. We could not understand why the driver turned so many times, or why he did not go straight to the place where we were to take the boat, for the conductor had told us the boat might be gone.

We became distrustful of the driver. We wondered why the conductor had asked us about our money and then had put us into this closed vehicle. We knew that the driver was not a conductor, nor a policeman, therefore he was not to be trusted. We felt sure he was taking us to some dark place in the city to rob us.

John had a small revolver which he took from his pocket, and after examining it, sat holding it in his hand ready for action.

"The first man that makes a move towards us, I will shoot him," John said.

Just then the driver turned into a broad, well lighted street. We saw a great many people coming from and going to a large, brilliantly lighted building which seemed to be right in the middle of the street. Our driver reined in his horses and told us to get out, which we very gladly did, for we did not trust him, and had not enjoyed the ride at all. He charged us two dollars, and we paid him; then he motioned us to enter the big building.

We didn't think that was the thing to do, but there we were on the street of a city, without a guide, no prospect of a boat, and no water in sight. I told John that we must find someone who could direct us, and we walked along the sidewalk to the corner of a great stone building, and there we saw a man in a blue uniform, a club in his hand, and a star on his coat, much to our joy. Out came our paper.

After reading the paper the policeman motioned us to follow him and he conducted us to the building into which the driver had motioned us to go. The policeman led us down some steps, into a large, well lighted room, with luxurious looking seats about, and told us to sit down, then disappeared up the steps. We waited, thinking he would return soon and take us to the boat. We were so anxious to reach our boat!

Presently we saw a man coming down the steps dressed like a conductor, but the word "Captain" was on his cap. However we felt that he was one who had authority, and out came our paper. After reading it, the captain smiled at us, bowed politely, and went on his way. We were almost in despair. Surely our boat would leave us, and we never would reach our destination.

Just then there was the most terrible, ear-splitting sound. It was somewhat like the whistle on the train, but even more terrible. Then the whole building began to move. Imagine our consternation. It began to dawn upon us that what we thought to be a building was a ship. We went across the room and looked out of a small window and could see nothing but water. We certainly were relieved. Once more we were on our journey.

Soon the captain returned. He was a very kind man and realized that we could understand all that he said to us. He showed us places where we might lie down safely and sleep, and explained to us that we would be very seasick if we sat up during the night. We were very tired and gladly welcomed a place of security where we might stretch out our stiff limbs and feel safe from molestation.

We did not fully appreciate the good captain's advice however, until a year or two later when we went with our battalion from Hampton Institute to Washington to attend the inauguration of President Garfield. On that occasion we went on a chartered steamer with General Armstrong and our commandant, Captain Roemain, who advised the boys to take to their bunks before we reached the ocean to avoid seasickness. We took no notice of his advice, and as a result we became the sickest lot of fellows imaginable and remained so until we reached land again. After that experience we fully appreciated the captain's advice, when he told us to lie down and sleep.

John and I arrived at Fortress Monroe about nine o'clock in the morning and were met there by General Armstrong, superintendent of Hampton Institute, with a carriage. A few minutes later we reached our destination, the school. Even yet the memory of that long journey seems more like a dream than an actual occurrence.

HAMPTON INSTITUTE

XIV

WHEN John King and I enrolled at Hampton Institute
it was as if we had entered a new world. Although
we had been accustomed to the regulations and discipline
of a government school at the Shawnee Indian boarding
school, yet in reality we knew nothing about the regulations
of such a school as Hampton Institute. It was a semi-military and industrial school; its rules and regulations were
strict and required promptness in their execution.

But the management was very lenient with us at the
beginning. For thirty days we were allowed absolute freedom from discipline and were encouraged to investigate
the campus and in fact the whole surrounding country. We
were allowed to fish in the James River and its bay en-
closure, which was fenced off near the school for that purpose. Everyone treated us kindly, and all that time we were
getting accustomed to the routine of the school and the
change in our habits.

Of the four or five hundred students, young men and
young women from all parts of the United States and
Cuba, fully one hundred were Indians. Though we were
the only Shawnee students, yet the presence of others of our
race made us feel more at ease. At the end of thirty days
we were assigned to our places in Company C of our battalion. Our regulations were similar to those in any well
organized military school of that time. From the time we
awakened at five o'clock in the morning almost every

moment of the day had its duties. We must prepare for breakfast in so many minutes, ready for roll call in our company, be ready at bugle call to march to the dining-room where we would stand at attention, boys on one side of the table and girls on the other, until a signal was given to seat ourselves. Twenty minutes were allowed for each meal.

After breakfast an hour of study began. Then we prepared our rooms for daily inspection. Our uniforms must be brushed properly and worn properly, and our shoes shined. Then a bugle called us to fall in line for another roll call after which came the morning inspection and military drill, before regular class work began. Every hour of the day had its duties; there was no shirking.

After supper there was a short evening prayer, accompanied by an instructive talk from the principal, which took place in the assembly room. A period of study lasted until nine o'clock, when we returned to our rooms to prepare for bed. At half past nine taps sounded, when lights must be out. This completed the day's work. We dressed, we ate, we drilled, we studied and recited our lessons with a precision that left not even one minute without its duties. No pupil was allowed to leave the campus without a pass from the proper officer. We learned to salute our teachers, our officers, and our fellow students with the proper respect. John King and I, who had so recently adopted the dress of the white man, had to learn to keep immaculate the uniform of the school, our linen spotless. Tooth brushes and bath tubs were conveniences we had to learn to use. It was all very strange to us, but we liked it. Only a short time elapsed before all these things came to us just as naturally as if we had practiced them always. As I have said before we had been trained to respect authority, and that is the secret of a successful apprenticeship to military life.

Hampton being a coeducational school, there was a certain amount of social activity between the boys and girls. We met the girls every day in the dining-room and in some classes, and we saw them in church, and there was a kind of good-fellowship between the sexes that was new to John King and me. On an average of once a month there was some kind of social entertainment in which the boys and girls met under proper supervision of teachers and officers. There was dancing, games, contests of different kinds, and conversation at these social affairs. Dancing was a favorite diversion for many of the young people. Some danced quadrilles and Virginia reels; there were some who danced waltzes and polkas; and there were some fine examples of solo dancing, such as the fisher's hornpipe, the Highland fling, and others. That kind of dancing was entirely new to John King and me, and at first we looked on in amazement. (We could have given them a warrior's dance if we had desired to do so.)

However, after we had become accustomed to the ways of the school and the comradeship of the young people, we took great pleasure in these social affairs. We liked the music, which was entirely new. We liked the games we learned to play, the contests of wit and humor. The association with the opposite sex on a footing of equality was something new, and I am afraid we were very crude and awkward at first. But the mutual exchange of ideas, the sympathy and encouragement we received from our teachers, their politeness and dignity, helped us to understand this phase of civilization, which was as delightful as it was new to us. I shall always remember with deep gratitude the kindly, pleasant efforts of my teachers to help me set myself right.

At Hampton we were taught the usages of polite society in vogue at that time, the so-called Victorian era (which is quite different from the "hail fellow well met" attitude of young people today), and in this we found the foundation of good breeding to be just the same principle as the simple teaching of our own people, namely, consideration for the rights of others, respect for our superiors (elders), and unselfishness. There were different ways of expressing this principle which is considered social culture, and which I contend is after all only the difference in social ethics. We were not taught by our people to make a pretense of esteem, where none existed, but in polite society we must conceal our real feelings, be they too affectionate, or too obnoxious. In short, etiquette is just an outward and uniform method of expressing courtesy. We slowly absorbed all these things and the practices of the social system at the school. John and I each found a young lady, who made delightful companions on those social occasions I have mentioned.

The young lady who became my partner was a beautiful Indian girl, a member of the Sioux tribe from South Dakota. We found that we had many ideas in common, as well as some problems, and we took up the white people's way of talking them over together. We both were ambitious and anxious to make the most of our opportunities. With such a sympathetic and interested listener, I learned to talk freely of my hopes and plans for the future. It was not very long until all my plans for the future included the presence of the young lady herself. I could see what a great and important work we might do together, after our school days were over, and she entered into the scheme heartily, after we had confessed our affection for each other.

I remember one experience that we had together that was very enjoyable. Although I never learned to dance after the fashion of the young people at the school I greatly enjoyed what was called "the promenade," which was simply a form of marching. We selected partners, just as if to dance, then while the orchestra played a march we slowly walked around the dance floor, keeping time to the music, the young lady's hand resting lightly on the arm of her escort. Occasionally judges were appointed, and prizes awarded to those who showed the most grace and who kept step with the music most accurately. On the night I mention this young lady and I were together and so pleasantly occupied with our conversation that we lost all thought of those about us, or the prize, and were most agreeably surprised when our names were called out before the assembly as winners of the prize, amid much clapping and merriment of the students, over our being so completely absorbed in each other.

The prize was an immense cake, beautifully decorated, which the young lady immediately cut into thin slices, so that as many of our friends as possible might share it. There was much merriment as they teased us about our absorbed manner while marching.

One day at Hampton I received a letter from one of the teachers at the Shawnee Mission school which contained an affidavit made by Robert Deer that my name was Alford. I liked the white man's way of taking his father's name, and had enrolled under the name of Thomas Wildcat. The name Thomas was given me by a very good friend, and I wanted to keep that, yet I wanted to do what was right and proper in the matter, so I took the letter to Miss Folsom, who was my adviser, and asked her advice. After due consideration, Miss Folsom said: "If I were you, I would not give up my own name, but just add this one to it." Thus my difficulty was solved, and thereafter I signed my name Thomas Wildcat Alford.

WHITE MAN'S RELIGION

XV

HAMPTON was not a sectarian school, yet there was a strong moral and religious influence ever working among the students. A short religious service was held daily in the assembly hall, and attendance at some church on the Sabbath was compulsory. Those who had church preferences were allowed to attend the church of their choice, but the regular school chapel service was of a union nature, and no church doctrine was taught.

It was not long before John King and I began to feel this religious influence. One of our teachers, Miss Cleveland, seemed to take especial interest in this side of our development and spent much time with us, even detaining us after Sunday school to talk to us and tell us the advantages of Christianity.

We enjoyed the study of the Bible, and found many instances where the teachings set forth in the great Book were similar to those of our own people. For instance the fifth verse of the twenty-fifth chapter of Deuteronomy reads: "If brethren dwell together, and one of them die, and have no son, the wife of the dead shall not be married unto a stranger." This practice of the old Jews was practically the same as among the Shawnee Indians up to the time of the opening of Oklahoma, when tribal laws gave way to state laws.

John and I often joked about this matter, before we were convinced that the Christian religion was better than our own. We jokingly promised each other that whoever of us died first and left a family, the other would marry his widow and rear his children as his own. But when we came to the more serious affairs of life we never thought anything about this promise, and in fact it was forgotten for the time.

Right here I shall tell of the continual struggle that went on in my soul about this question of religion which was to play such an important part in my life and was to bring such bitter disappointments. For a time after I went to Hampton this matter did not disturb me at all. It did not occur to me that I would ever care to break the promise I had made my uncle Big Jim concerning my acceptance of the Christian faith. I planned continually for the time when I would return to the West and take up my work among my own people. Every day I took up some new idea or gained a broader view of life, and the thought would come to me, "now I can teach that to my people," or that "this knowledge or that idea will be of advantage to me when I become chief of the Shawnees." These thoughts gave me courage to endure many an hour of homesickness when every atom of my being was crying out for a glimpse of the dear, familiar faces of my family and friends, or the rest and quiet of a day in my native country, listening to the music of the woods and the messages the wind whispered among the trees.

But as time passed and the interest of my teachers became stronger, their pleas more insistent, I could not ignore the subject. I began to consider the religious beliefs and to study the Gospel of Jesus Christ. At first this did not seem to be a different religion to our own, in a way, but just a better way of teaching or of understanding the belief of my own people. It really seemed to explain things that I had never been able to see clearly. The mental processes by which we were able to grasp religious beliefs were exactly

[105]

the same. Religion is in no instance a tangible thing that can be explained by some philosophical process, but always is to be explained by faith in an unseen power. To an Indian mind, one who can and does believe in the existence of a Supreme Spirit and in the close association of nature and a human being, some kind of religion is necessary. I had been taught that man was created in the image of the Great Spirit, his creator, and that he was personally responsible for every word and act, thought or deed. The continual presence of a guiding Spirit was also an acknowledged similarity in our beliefs, but there it ended.

Under the continual pressure and interest of my friends and teachers, this question of religion became a paramount issue in my mind. I became conscious of a deep soul hunger to know the truth. Then came the conviction of the truth, the dawn of knowledge, when I knew deep in my soul that Jesus Christ was my Savior.

But very well did I know that when I accepted this faith I renounced virtually all hope to be a ruler, a chief of my people. What did it matter if I knew ever so much that would be good for my people, if I never was allowed to guide or lead them? Then there was the matter of personal ambition. No young white man ever had more ambition to be a governor of his state than I had to be chief of my people. The people we know and love make up our world, be they great or simple. The Shawnee Indians are my people; they make up my world.

This struggle went on continually. There was no rest from these thoughts and no quieting of the insistent voice that was ever calling in my heart, calling me to the feet of Jesus. In the end that voice won, and I was happy in the love of God, although very well I knew that my hope of earthly glory was over—my dream had been in vain. I could work for my people, I might even teach them the truth about

Christianity, but they never would accord to me the honor and respect they gave to their chief. Time has proven this to be true.

This question of religion being settled to my satisfaction, and that of my teachers and friends, I was able to concentrate on my studies. That I succeeded in making a place for myself in the activities of the school is proved by a number of honors that were conferred upon me. I am sure that I had the respect and confidence of my teachers and officers.

When I first entered school and was allowed to select some occupation to work at during my spare time, whereby to help pay my expenses, I had taken up work at a sawmill that was operated by the school. But I got my finger badly cut by the saw, and was transferred to the printing office where I remained as long as I stayed there. I quickly learned to set type and to do almost any of the work that was to be done in the shop, thereby earning a small sum that helped materially with my expenses.

Miss Alice Longfellow, who had offered the scholarship which had been awarded to me, had shown a personal interest in my progress, and wrote to me occasionally. Her letters were a great encouragement and inspiration to me. She held up to me the great responsibility that was mine to do something for my people. Especially did she urge me to use my influence to improve the condition of Indian women and girls. After I left Hampton and was teaching school, she urged me to see that Indian girls had the same advantages that were enjoyed by boys in my school.

In company with other students I made several trips to eastern cities. One that I already have mentioned was the one to Washington to witness the inauguration of President Garfield. I was flag sergeant at that time, and had the honor of tipping the flag to the President. During my senior year I went with General Armstrong and two or three other students as representative of the Indian students at Hampton, to New York, Philadelphia, Boston, and other large cities. The object of this tour was to interest the people in the education of the Indians and in helping Hampton Institute in a financial way. I made speeches on the educational needs of our people. We succeeded in raising a large sum of money, sixty thousand dollars, I believe.

While we were in New York City General Armstrong, James Murry, a Pawnee Indian, and I were invited to the home of a very nice lady, whose name I do not recall. She had a beautiful home, in fact more elegant than I ever had seen before. She had a wonderful collection of paintings, and entertained us by explaining her pictures. Then she took us into her drawing-room where she served tea. When we left she presented me with a beautiful gold watch, the first I ever had owned.

While in New York we stopped at a hotel called The Porter House.[1] One day James and I went out to see the sights of the city, and because we did not take the trouble to notice the way we took, we became lost. We retraced our steps, but the houses all seemed to look alike. We were utterly bewildered. But finally we saw a policeman, and having a great respect for a man with a club in his hand and a star on his coat, we asked him to direct us back to our hotel, and returned without unpleasant adventure.

General Armstrong gave us a lecture about keeping our directions, but did not scold us unnecessarily. The trip was a very delightful one to me, for it revealed many things that I had read about and could not understand. In other words, it enlarged my vision.

Three years in an eastern school brought about a great change in both my feelings and my appearance. I had

1. The Porter House in New York City was at that time considered the finest hotel in America. It was from it that Porter House steak got its name.

learned those little details of toilet that were considered essential to the dress of "a civilized man." In fact, John King often laughed at what he considered my extreme habit of neatness, and accused me of being "a regular dude." I no longer felt awkward or self-conscious when in the society of the opposite sex. I had learned those outward forms of manner that give one a comfortable feeling when in the company of well-bred people. Education had not made me critical or supercilious, but it had opened my mind and heart to a broader understanding of the human race and a greater love and appreciation of my own people. I felt a yearning desire to impart to them some of the good and pleasant things I had learned. They were missing so many things that they might enjoy, so many privileges they might claim. There was such a broad field to work in. I was eager to get back home and take up my work with them.

At the time I graduated there were a great many notable people present—men and women who took a leading part in the philanthropical and educational activities of the country. Many of them were known to me and had encouraged me in my desire to be of service. At the graduating exercise I made a talk telling of my experience at the school, what it had meant to me, and how I intended to use my education and my life for the benefit of my people.

So ended my school days.

HOME AGAIN—DISAPPOINTMENTS

XVI

MY RETURN journey was very different from the trip to the East three years before. I was alone, for John King had not completed the course he was taking at Hampton and remained a year or two longer than I did.

I no longer thought it necessary to carry a "paper" to identify me and to explain my destination, nor was I dependent upon the conductor or some other uniformed person to direct me about. I did not hesitate to enter into conversation with my fellow passengers who showed a friendly interest in me. I had grown accustomed to seeing well cultivated farms and beautiful country places, as well as thriving cities. As our train sped westward and the towns we passed became smaller and smaller, the country homes poorer and more isolated, I felt an odd sense of disappointment. I had not realized that the country I had left behind me had changed so little. In fact I had forgotten how wonderful those same towns had seemed to me when I saw them for the first time.

I left the train at Tulsa, having taken a different route to the one I had used when we went East. Tulsa was only a small town then, but I happened to meet Charley, a Shawnee whose wife Betsey was a distant relative of my mother. He lived about twelve miles from Tulsa, and I went home with him to spend the night. The next day I took the mail stage to Shawnee Town, where I arrived in due time.

My homecoming was a bitter disappointment to me. Noticing at once the change in my dress and manner, in my speech and conduct, my people received me coldly and with suspicion. Almost at once they suspected that I had taken up the white man's religion, along with his habits and manner of conduct. There was no happy gathering of family and friends, as I had so fondly dreamed there might be. Instead of being eager to learn the new ideas I had to teach them, they gave me to understand very plainly that they did not approve of me. I had no real home to go to, and my relatives did not welcome my presence.

I answered my people by associating myself with the missionary, the Reverend Franklin Elliot. I had no one to go to for advice, save my white friends Blossom and Clay, and the employees at the boarding school.

I missed sorely the comforts and conveniences I had grown accustomed to at Hampton, and very, very much I missed the happy association with my classmates and friends. The young Sioux girl I have mentioned had been very kind to me during those last months we had been together at Hampton. In fact when we parted she promised me that when I was ready, she would take up the duties of life with me. This promise had made me very happy at the time it was given, but after I had returned to my people and had been so coldly received I doubted the wisdom of asking her to come here to share the hardships and suffer the disappointments that would inevitably fall to our lot. However her letters to me were very cheering, and so were those of some other friends and teachers, who wrote to me regularly after receiving my announcement of a safe arrival at home.

After the first disappointment of homecoming was over I began to look about for work. Being so eager to work and to use the knowledge I had labored so hard to acquire, it was a keen disappointment when I could find no lucrative opening.

Reverend Elliot employed me as interpreter, which was very gratifying in a way, for it gave me a chance to talk to the Indians about the religious life I had found so satisfying. It also gave me an opportunity to tell them something about the ways of civilization, and most of all it really did bring me into contact with them. But the remuneration was pitifully small, and I felt that I was capable of doing something much better, where my work might reach many more people. But I remained with this work until I had saved up a little money for expenses, and then I set out to find a position.

I went on horseback to the Cheyenne and Arapahoe Agency, then located at Darlington (now Canadian County, Oklahoma), hoping to find employment there. At Darlington I met Reverend H. R. Voth of the Mennonite Mission, from whom I afterwards received several interesting letters about missionary work among the Indians. But I failed to get work there, and I resolved to go on to Anadarko to the Kiowa, Comanche, and Wichita Agency to see an old classmate at Hampton, John Downing. But I failed to see John and could not find any promise of work, so I decided to return home again.

I bought a piece of barbecued meat and some bread from the Indians, which I put in my saddlebag (which Reverend Elliot had kindly lent me with his horse and saddle), and started back home. I took a course northeast and traveled over an unknown route, stopping to camp at night wherever I could find water, when night seemed to be overtaking me. I arrived in Shawnee Town, tired out and utterly discouraged.

My old employers, Blossom and Clay, had dissolved partnership, but Mr. Clay still was in the community, and when

I had failed to get any kind of work he offered me a ride in his buggy with him into Kansas. I gladly accepted his offer, hoping to get work in a printing office at Lawrence, Kansas.

It took us three days to reach Arkansas City, which then was only a village of one street, a store in which there was a post office, with a few houses clustered about it, mostly farm houses and barns. We spent one night there, and the next day turned our course towards Wamego, where we parted. Mr. Clay visited his brother who lived there, and I took the train to Lawrence and then to other towns, seeking employment, but failed to find anything to do.

However, I had a very pleasant visit with a former teacher of mine, Miss Ella D. Coltrane, who then lived near Lawrence, Kansas. She now is a practicing physician at Ada, Oklahoma. She had been a teacher at the Shawnee Boarding School while I was a student there.

I finally returned to Shawnee Town by stage, "dead broke, without a job," and thoroughly discouraged. I had thought it would be easy to get some kind of work, but I had found it very difficult, indeed.

I had applied soon after I came home to J. V. Carter, Indian Agent at the Sauk and Fox Agency, for a place in the Shawnee Boarding School. The Shawnees, Pottawatomies, Kickapoos, and Iowas were all under that Agency then, and all business between the government and any of those tribes or members of the tribes was transacted at that Agency. I failed to get that position, but it led to my assignment as teacher for a Pottawatomie Indian day school, just when I had begun to think there was nothing but disappointment in store for me.

THE YOUNG SCHOOL TEACHER

XVII

THE Pottawatomie school to which I was assigned was at a place called Wa-go-za located about three miles west of the present town of Wanette, Oklahoma, near a Pottawatomie Indian village.

The school building was a log cabin about 12x14 feet; the cracks between the logs were filled with red clay, which shut out the cold wind. The floor was made of rough split timber, and the two windows were without glass or shutters. It stood in a thick wood of post oak timber.

My school opened there November 1, 1882, which was the date of my entrance into the U. S. Indian Service that was to last for many years, off and on. In fact, it has been my life work and has given me many advantages and opportunities to help my own people.

A day or two before school opened I found a white man named Billy Trousdale in a blacksmith shop near Shawnee Town, with whom I secured a ride out to his farm, about eighteen miles in the direction of my school. He had married a Pottawatomie woman named Toupin. I spent the night with Mr. Trousdale, and started walking the remaining distance to my school, about seven miles, early the next morning. I carried a small parcel which contained my clothing, and in my hand I carried the "striking clock" which had been a gift to me from one of my teachers, Miss Fletcher, when I left school. This clock was looked upon as a wonder by my pupils.

[114]

I engaged board with a family of white people named Wilson who rented land from a Citizen Pottawatomie named John Anderson, whose land adjoined the Indian village. There I lived through the school term. They were very nice people to be with. Mr. Wilson told me he was a "hard-shell Baptist," but I did not know the difference between a hard-shell and a soft-shell of his denomination, so I was not much the wiser for the volunteered information. He often tried to argue Scriptures or church doctrine, but I didn't care to argue, and would switch the conversation by telling him some old Indian legend. Then he would open his mouth, and sit and listen attentively and forget his hard-shell notions. I got along very well with this family while I taught there, and kept their table supplied with game.

I enjoyed my work with my pupils too. They were mostly boys between the ages of twelve and sixteen years. All of them could speak English, and were intelligent in their way. We spent much of our time hunting, on Saturdays and holidays, for the country abounded in turkeys and other small game.

Here I will relate an experience that afforded me a great deal of amusement after it was over, but seemed tragic enough while we were going through it.

Mr. Wilson had a son about fourteen years old who was one of my pupils. One evening we decided that we would go for a turkey hunt by moonlight. They owned a shotgun which was the largest in caliber I ever saw. Mr. Wilson had named it "the bone trigger" because its original trigger was broken or lost, and he had shaped a hard bone and fitted it into the place of the original trigger. This was the gun we had to carry whenever we hunted.

On this particular night we passed through a strip of woods and a small prairie, at the farther end of which was a deep, dry ravine, which we crossed and again entered the woods where we believed a flock of turkeys roosted. Sure enough, we found the roost and shot one turkey and a buzzard which we mistook for a turkey, on account of the moon being obscured by a heavy cloud that came rolling up from the northwest. We decided to wait a while until the cloud had passed, so that we could see our way. We made a fire to warm ourselves, for it was growing very cold. But instead of the cloud passing a storm broke, rain came in sheets, with piercing lightning and bursting thunder. We decided to run for home. The Wilson boy took the turkey, and I took the bone trigger.

With what light we could get from the almost constant flashes of lightning we tried to retrace our steps homeward. The rain and wind beat in our faces, and our clothing was so wet we could hardly walk. Soon we came to what we believed to be the neighborhood of the dry ravine we had crossed such a short time before. But we were nearer than we thought, and partially blinded by lightning flashes I stumbled, stepped over the bank, and down I went into the ravine, now full of swift-running icy-cold water. Before I could warn my companion who was following close at my heels, he too came tumbling in after me.

In the scramble we lost both the turkey and the bone trigger. But fortunately we were not frightened by the plunge and soon recovered our luggage and were on our way home again. To say that we were wet to the skin, and cold, doesn't sufficiently describe our condition, for we were thoroughly soaked and chilled. However we had a lot of fun telling about our escapade.

While I taught at Wa-go-za I had a great deal of spare time, and I corresponded regularly with several friends I had made at Hampton, though our mails were not very regular, being carried on horseback for a long distance. I especially value a letter I received from my benefactress,

Miss Longfellow. Always in her letters to me Miss Longfellow had emphasized the idea that I should be of great benefit to my people. Now when she heard that I was teaching school she suggested again that I try to improve the educational opportunity of Indian girls. As this was one of the principles of our own family, it was easy enough for me to carry out her theories, as far as it lay in my power to do so. Indian girls were slow to take advantage of such opportunities, because they had been taught from infancy that boys were the first to be considered.

Another correspondence that I especially enjoyed that winter was with the dear young lady whom I have mentioned before, the Sioux Indian girl from South Dakota, whom I had learned to love while at Hampton. In fact, it was her letters and her cheerful way of writing to me that had kept up my courage and caused me to make more earnest efforts in all worthwhile things during those gloomy days after I returned from Hampton and found myself excluded from the love and confidence of my people. Indeed, at times I was utterly cast down, for it seemed that my tribe had ostracized me, and I never again would have their affection. All during that long winter we wrote to each other regularly, and it seemed that we were in a fair way to realize our dream of an early date for our marriage. I saved my money, and was beginning to plan for our home.

I taught only one school year at Wa-go-za, and then was transferred to the government boarding school for the Shawnees, as principal. My future looked very bright. At last I was to be in a position where I would have an opportunity to do something for my people. I realized that I would not have the influence with the older people that I coveted, but wouldn't it be far better to direct the education of the young? Would I not be able to instill into their plastic young minds and hearts some of the good things I had learned while at Hampton? I believed that I would.

Then this promise of a permanent position meant soon I would be able to bring the young lady of my choice to help me in my life work! I was very happy over the prospects. Imagine my surprise and dismay, then, to receive a letter from the pastor of the young lady making a strong objection to our marriage on denominational grounds. It seemed that the pastor had the idea that if the young lady separated herself from his particular church that her soul's salvation would be forfeited. He took it for granted that when she married me she would adopt my church affiliations and renounce his.

I cannot to this day understand the position of the man. I had met him once and he seemed to be a very scholarly man. But his letter made a lasting impression on my mind, and caused me to form an antipathy against ministers who seek to dominate the members of their churches. I had been taught to believe that God alone is the source of salvation, and I could not reconcile myself to this man's idea. Religion and church doctrines were so new to me that I did not feel myself capable of arguing the question with the reverend gentleman. I will say here however, that after many years of close study of the Scriptures I still am unable to find anything to justify his attitude.

I had believed the young lady would be of great benefit to my people, as well as a constant inspiration to me. She seemed to combine a very charming personality with a fund of practical common sense. She was highly accomplished, earnest, and energetic. We were very congenial, and she understood perfectly my attitude toward my work and my life. She always had seemed to approve all my plans.

It was a terrible blow to all my plans and hopes. But as I did not want to do anything to endanger the salvation or the happiness of the girl I loved (the minister had said both would be placed in jeopardy), like a true Indian, I decided to forego my own happiness for her good. I so notified her, and after considerable futile correspondence, we decided that we each should go our own way, and a spirit of warm friendliness is all that has existed between us since.

She was married to a white man not very long afterwards, with the approval of her pastor, I presume. I have never seen her since we parted at Hampton. So ended my first love affair.

THE BIRD'S NEST

XVIII

I HAD little time for grieving after the incidents mentioned in the last chapter, had I been inclined to indulge in vain regrets and memories. Although I was sadly disappointed, the work that was before me was still the paramount interest in my life, and I would not let personal desires interfere with its execution. I might say that the association with my white friends at the Mission, especially the Reverend Franklin Elliot and his family, prevented the shock I had received from upsetting my faith in church people. My faith in God never wavered, for it amounted to personal knowledge and understanding. Denominational bickering is something that never has been excusable in my judgment, although it seems a favorite pastime for many so-called Christians. Queer civilization!

After I returned to Shawnee Town and had received the appointment for the government school, I set myself to the task of winning back the confidence of my people. This was not so difficult as it had been a year ago, for they were beginning to see that my desire to serve them was as strong as it had been when they sent me away to school. Not for a moment did they ever allow me to think or even hope that I might become their chief, yet they cautiously and timidly began to talk to me about tribal matters. Finding that my adoption of religion had not changed my interest in tribal affairs, they gradually and guardedly gave me their confidence. They were beginning to see that the change in my manner and dress had not changed my feelings. I had been with them a year, and they could find no reason to doubt the sincerity and earnestness of my desire to give them the benefit of what I had learned.

In all my talks with the Indians I lost no opportunity to tell them the advantages of education, and though I had to use much diplomacy, I advised them to send their children to school. The direct result of this, and other influences working along the same line, was that a much larger number of Indians made application for their children to enter boarding school that year.

I was full of ideas for teaching, eager to try out some of the newer methods I had learned at Hampton. In this I had the encouragement of the missionaries and the Indian agent.

Already a great change had taken place in the country. Many white people had come into Indian Territory under one pretext or another. All over the United States there was talk of opening the unoccupied lands for white settlement, and some even suggested that the whole Indian Territory should be thrown open. Rumors like these reached the ears of the Indians, which caused restlessness and dissatisfaction, that reached even into the schoolroom.

About the time that I returned to Shawnee Town from Wa-go-za John King came home from Hampton, and our reunion was a great pleasure to us both. He brought me news, fresh from all my friends at Hampton, and we were able to sustain each other in our efforts to hold fast the things we had learned.

Some of John's relatives had died and left him some property; he opened a store at Shawnee Town about the time that I opened the school. He tried to furnish our people with the necessities of a better mode of living, while I was striving to prepare them for civilization and citizenship.

My school opened September 1, 1883, with the largest enrolment there ever had been, and it soon was apparent that the buildings were not adequate to accommodate the number of pupils. Besides, I had made plans for the school that would necessitate some vocational buildings. Application was made through the proper channels that resulted in the enlargement of the school and many improvements in the buildings. The work, however, was not started until early in the following spring. I had to close the school while the work was going forward.

But before I had closed the school I was delighted to have a visit from my old white chief, General Armstrong. He was making a tour of the country visiting the graduates of his school, to see for himself what they were doing for their people—to ascertain just how his plan of *service* was working. He congratulated me heartily on the work I was doing and my management of the school, and at the same time offered some suggestions for improvement from his own fertile brain. He left me with renewed courage and determination. While my school was closed, and I was temporarily idle there was a council held by the Shawnees in which they decided to send me as a delegate, with two others, to Washington to present to the Commissioner of Indian Affairs their desire that Little River be made the permanent southern boundary of their land. This had been a vexing question ever since the Pottawatomies had come among us.

We found when we had an interview with the Commissioner that it would take an act of Congress to make the boundary permanent, and remembering other experiences with Congress we returned without success.

After I returned from Washington I spent a good deal of my time while waiting for the school buildings to be completed, at the Sauk and Fox Agency, and in visiting the school there. One of the teachers, Miss Mary Grinnell, was a sister-in-law of the Reverend Franklin Elliot who had proven himself such a dependable friend to me. She was the daughter of Reverend Jeremiah A. Grinnell, a prominent minister in the Society of Friends, and felt a deep interest in Indians generally.

I had known Miss Grinnell for a long time, having seen her at the home of Reverend and Mrs. Elliot on my frequent visits there and on my occasional visits to the Sauk and Fox Agency. We had a great many problems in common, both being interested in the advancement of our pupils, and the cause of civilization in general. This mutual sympathy and friendship gradually ripened into a deeper feeling, and we "became engaged" as young people say these days.

I at once set about building a home, for there was no provision made at the school for the family of the principal. There was a beautiful location for a house on my land about one-third of a mile distant from the school, and there we decided to build our home. I lost no time in getting the work started on the building, clearing the ground with my own hands. I had accumulated enough money to pay for the material, and what help I would have to hire. (I wanted to do just as much of the work as I could myself.)

All the framework of the house was made of native oak timber, hewn by hand from trees that grew on the place, but the pine lumber used was hauled from Atoka, a point on the railroad nearly a hundred miles distant. I took a number of men with wagons to Atoka to get the lumber, and the trip took nearly a week. I remember that the hauling of the lumber amounted to more than the price of the lumber at the yard.

My old friend, Mr. Blossom, was in business at Atoka at that time and I had a long talk with him, while waiting for my men to load their wagons. He was surprised and pleased too when I told him that I was to be married to Miss Grinnell. He congratulated me heartily and wished us much happiness.

When all the material was on the ground I hired my friend John Paden to help me with the building. We had great oak sills ten inches square, cut from the hearts of trees for the foundation. Every piece of timber used was personally selected. All our friends were interested, and watched the development of the house with keen enjoyment.

When finished the house was 24x12, not very large, but it was large enough. There were two rooms, one was living room and bedroom combined, the other one served for kitchen and dining-room, and was considered an unusually good house for that time. Clean, new, comfortable, furnished simply, yet tastefully, it presented an ideal appearance to me and to the lovely lady who had consented to make her home there with me.

Dear old Aunty Kirk, wife of the missionary, Reverend J. A. Kirk—both beloved by all Indians who knew them—called our home "The Bird's Nest" and that name it bears today, although for many years a much larger and more commodious structure has taken the place of the original one.

When my home was finished and all the arrangements completed, an invitation was given to all our friends and neighbors to attend a service at the little white mission church. After the usual Sunday morning service, Brother Elliot led us with all our friends to a little grove immediately south of the church and there he consummated our union, September 7, 1884.

After congratulations from all present, the meeting broke up, and I led my beautiful "White Bird" home to the "Nest" I had built for her.

THE SHAWNEE BOARDING SCHOOL

XIX

THE work on the boarding school progressed slowly. All the material had to be hauled a long distance, over rough roads, and then as now work on government property had a way of "dragging."

I was very anxious to be at work, and took for a short time a position at the Chillocco Indian school, but my wife did not enjoy the situation there, so I resigned, and we returned to our home, where always there was plenty of work to be done.

I resumed my work in the Shawnee Boarding School in February, 1885. The new buildings and improvements enabled me to carry out some of my theories about teaching Indian children, though the school was poorly equipped for the work I tried to do. There were between forty and fifty pupils, and I had only one assistant, besides the matron.

It must be remembered that Indian children of that time had to be taught the very rudiments of civilization, as well as to speak and read the English language. Such simple things as the use of chairs to sit on, the correct way to eat at a table, the use of knives and forks, the care of their beds such as spreading sheets properly, all had to be taught the children. Then they had to be taught habits of personal neatness, such as regular baths, the care of teeth, the brushing of their hair, and habits of decorum. In many cases it was much more difficult to teach them these things than it was to teach them to speak and read English, for civilized manners were things considered utterly unnecessary by the parents of the children, and they were not encouraged to take up such ways.

My greatest desire was to teach the boys to work, and to instill into their minds their responsibility towards their families. Many generations of ancestors who believed that the women of the tribe should do all the heavy labor had left their imprint on the character of the Indians in what seemed to be an indelible stamp. The women and girls accepted the situation without protest, and of course the boys believed as their fathers did, although they were not lazy. They would hunt or play games that called for great strength and endurance, yet would sit down contentedly and allow the women of their households to do the manual labor. I tried to inculcate habits of industry, and to teach them the advantages of regular work. I especially tried to teach them a better way of farming, and to be more skilful with the hammer and saw, and to do their own blacksmith work. It was not an easy task, and it called for unlimited patience and perseverance.

The girls likewise were taught the rudiments of home-making: to do plain neat sewing, to cook and serve food properly. Even the homely task of dishwashing—the bug-bear of girls universally I am told—had to be taught to the girls of our school. Dishwashing was almost unknown in the primitive Indian family, for the simple reason that very few of them had any dishes to wash. All these things had to be taught the children who came to our school, because it was to be a part of their civilization.

I tried to keep in close contact with my pupils, to win and hold their confidence, and to impress upon their minds the importance of education and the advantages of civilization. I did this in school and out of school, being careful always not to allude to their home environment, or to seem to be critical of their old way of living. Like them I had been ignorant of all these things, and I was in a position to sympathize with them. I could in reality "speak their language" and understand their problems.

Memories of those days are still a pleasure to me. Busy, happy, useful days when I could see the results of my work in the development of the children under my care. Most of the children quickly took up the life at the school, learned their lessons, respected our teaching. Indeed, it was remarkable how quickly they adapted themselves to the new environment even before they could speak the language.

Isaac A. Taylor was Indian Agent at that time, and he approved all my plans and gave substantial support to my undertakings. The Friends' missionaries helped too, with untiring zeal. My young wife, herself a born teacher and missionary, was a constant inspiration and help to me in all that I tried to do.

Many of my pupils of those days have become successful men and women in different fields of endeavor. Some have won distinction in their chosen work and a great many are good, law abiding citizens. Whether this has been the result of my work or of those who came after me, does not matter in the least. I did my best and most of the teachers who have been in the school have done the same. But it does give me a thrill of pride and thankfulness to realize that my efforts helped start my people on their way to civilization and citizenship.

I taught in the school five years, and even after I no longer was connected with it, my interest in my pupils did not cease. My work led me into other fields of endeavor, where there seemed to be greater need, but from time to time I came in contact with my former pupils, and often I was able to be of service to them, which always was a great pleasure to me. I still come in contact with some of them, and am glad to say that they generally are holding dependable places and are doing their bit of the world's work. Many of them have gone on their long journey, while I still am carrying on.

During those early years of my experience in the government employ, teachers and other employees of the Indian service had considerable trouble holding their positions because of the "political spoils" system. Capability, efficiency, or fitness had little to do with securing an appointment, and I am sorry to say that very often little consideration was shown for the real welfare of the Indians when agents or teachers were appointed. Indian agents, special agents, and teachers for the Indian schools generally were appointed to repay election promises, and were discharged when some other successful candidate needed the place to satisfy some of his loyal supporters. Men who had no training or special interest in Indian work often were given positions of great responsibility, places made vacant by the discharge of some conscientious workers who truly were interested in their charges. Some agent or teacher would formulate a plan that might have resulted in great good, when snap! Off would go his head, or at least his job, and someone would be put into his place who had neither knowledge of nor interest in his work.

I was no exception to this rule. My wife and I were specially trained for the Indian service, and we gave to our work the best that was in us—but we never knew when we would be discharged, or for what reason. For instance, one year we were living at Bird's Nest, our home adjoining the school grounds, since there was no provision made at the school for our quarters. A crowded condition actually existed there, and we were near enough to be on duty constantly, but a certain special agent reported that I was not living on the school premises, and under this flimsy excuse obtained my removal as principal of the school and had the place given to a friend of his. However, in this one instance justice prevailed. I soon was reinstated, and finished the term, after which I resigned. This finished my career in the schoolroom.

While I have not been connected directly with the school since that time, I never have ceased to hold a deep interest in the institution. I know that the school and the Friends' Mission adjoining have been the largest factors in the civilization of our people.

Too much credit cannot be given to the teachers who have labored at the school, for in the early days of the institution the work entailed unspeakable hardships and privations. The teachers were required to live at the school, to be constantly associated with the pupils, and to share with the children its meager and pitifully inadequate accommodations. The allowances for food always were much too little. There were no available markets; no cows were kept at the school; and very few vegetables were grown after I left. In fact there were scarcely any vegetables grown in the country, and scarcely any fruit. All supplies had to be hauled a long distance. A new railroad had gone through Oklahoma country by that time, with a station—Oklahoma Station—some fifty miles distant, and supplies were hauled from there or from Muskogee or Atoka. The roads were rough, and there were no bridges over the rivers or creeks. In winter there was no passing for months at a time.

Beef was furnished and killed at the Sauk and Fox Agency, and the supply generally was plentiful. Tallow was the only shortening used. Canned milk, bread flour, beans, dried apples, and a very few cases of canned goods, vegetables, and fish, with coffee and tea were the rations provided for the school. Even potatoes were scarce and a great treat when they could be had.

[130]

At one time there was no water supply at the school. From some cause the well had failed, and all the water used by the school had to be hauled from the North Canadian River about one mile distant. Even then the supply was very limited, because there was no provision made for hauling the water, no tanks or casks for the purpose, no one who could be spared to do the work. No provision was made for sanitation or conveniences, except of the crudest kind.

One of the former teachers at the school, recently speaking of the hardships she endured while teaching there, told some pathetic stories. She said the water from the river they had to use was so brackish and foul looking that she could not bear to drink it, and lived for months by drinking only tea at meal time. In tea, she could forget the condition of the water before being boiled. She said the children were bathed—it was a part of the teachers' duties to help the children with their baths—in huge washtubs; the smallest were bathed first, then the larger ones, as long as the water could possibly be used. Even then it was saved to mop the floors with.

Teachers were paid quarterly at the rate of fifty dollars a month, but they had to pay their board out of that sum. However, their board was limited to the actual cost of the food, as nearly as it could be estimated, and was not very much. One teacher reported that her board bill for three months was only $11.25.

Such conditions, such isolation, and such low salaries put teaching in the Indian schools on the same basis as missionary work, yet as I have explained the positions were sought eagerly, and often were peddled out through the political spoils system. However, I must say that at the time of which I am writing the whole country was going through a period of financial depression, when work was held up on all public projects, and money was terribly scarce. Even one's wildest dreams could not have pictured such prosperity as has since prevailed.

Notwithstanding all the hardships endured by the teachers, the school continued to function splendidly, and was recognized for the good work it was doing. From time to time additions were made to the buildings, and better equipment was furnished.

After the country was opened for white settlement a great change was wrought in the school, consistent with the development of the country, and the progress of the Indians. For it must not be forgotten that advancement was going forward along many lines, and even some of the older tribesmen were accepting the changes that were taking place, while many of the younger people had made places in the community for themselves.

But to return to the school. As the pupils advanced, and more and more were enrolled each year, a larger staff of teachers was employed and better facilities for vocational training were added. Home-making and domestic art received especial attention from the girls, and music was taught to all who would try to learn it. Many of our children developed talents that have won public recognition.

As the years passed, many deeply interested, seriously earnest teachers came to the school, each giving something peculiarly his own to the institution, leaving lasting impressions on the minds of the pupils. Who can say what these teachers, both men and women, have done for our race? Some of them have left the imprint of their fine natures, their true personalities on the lives of the children with whom they labored; their influence will live on and on, down through the ages, bearing rich fruit in the years to come. But at the time they were working among us, some of them failed to see any results of their labors and felt discouraged and worn with care.

Among those who taught at the Shawnee school during those early years when the hardships were grievous was Miss Harriet Patrick, daughter of Major Samuel Patrick, who was for many years agent at the Sauk and Fox Agency. She had lived most of her life at an Indian agency, and understood Indian character. She was known and loved by many of our people before she came among us as a teacher. She was married in 1899 to Harry B. Gilstrap, a man who now is known nationally for his work of rehabilitation among veterans of the World War.

Other teachers came, labored for a while, and passed on. The Society of Friends kept up their work of civilization, teaching a doctrine of peace and good will that appealed to the understanding of our people, but which it was hard to connect with the encroaching commercialism that was growing more pronounced every day.

And so I leave the story of the Shawnee Indian Boarding School for a time, to tell of my own work in another field.

ALLOTTING LAND TO THE SHAWNEES

XX

WHEN I gave up my work in the Shawnee Boarding School I felt that the older people of my tribe needed me more than the younger generation. Rumors that the country would be opened for white settlement had caused so much distress and unhappiness that I felt it my duty to spend much of my time with them, and it was impossible for me to do so and keep up my work in the schoolroom.

A great change already had come in the country. Many white people were scattered about, traders, cattle men, outlaws; and the Indians felt them to be a grave menace. Every newspaper that came into the country was read by these white men, and they would tell the Indians about efforts being made to have the Oklahoma land opened for homestead entry. In fact the so-called "Sooners" already were trying to settle in the northern part of the country, and it took all the vigilance of the troops scattered along the Kansas border to frustrate their designs.

Our people recalled former experiences when white men had wanted their land, and they knew very well that once the Oklahoma country was opened, it would be a matter of only a few years until the whole Indian Territory would be invaded. They would be asked to move on as their ancestors had been forced to do so many times. Full well they knew that there was no place left them to go. They had their backs to the wall. Opposed to civilization, opposed to the allotment of land in severalty, these brave, strong men were in a pitiable condition.

I gave most of my time to talking with them, singly or in groups. I tried to explain things to them, to interpret the news that I read in the papers truthfully, and to teach them to be resigned. I saw that the condition they dreaded was fast approaching—it was inevitable. The country soon would be divided, allotted, and they should adapt themselves to the change, and take up the ways of civilization.

I tried to induce them to plant and cultivate their land so they no longer would be dependent upon hunting and fishing for their subsistence. I urged them to work, to manage, to use business methods!

It was unfortunate for the Shawnees that in 1884 they lost their most progressive leader, as well as their most beloved chief, Joseph Ellis. Although he was almost blind in his later years, being more than ninety years old when he died, he was foremost in industry and in things that tended to improve living conditions among the people. He was the tribal historian and had kept clear in his memory the history and traditions of the Shawnee Nation. He had been esteemed as an orator and was respected and admired by the white men who knew him. He was a relative of our family, his mother Toh-si being the sister of my grandfather Se-leet-ka. He was called Uncle Joe by the white people.

In 1885 our principal chief, John Sparney, died. He also was an intelligent and progressive man; he was succeeded by White Turkey, whom many of the white settlers of this country still remember. The loss of these two progressive leaders left the Shawnees in a sad condition, subject as they were to the influence of those non-progressive chiefs Big Jim and Sam Warrior, both of whom fought bitterly against every form of civilization. They had never

[135]

become reconciled to the presence of the Pottawatomies among us, and ill feeling, dissension, and threatenings were heard on every side.

This condition called for constant watchfulness, and to a large degree I felt this responsibility rested upon me. Although I never would be their chief, I had been reared with that expectation and I felt that this would be one of my opportunities to serve them. I think now that I did help a little to prepare them for citizenship, but at the time it seemed to me that all my efforts were wasted; they would not see things as I tried to make them see.

The Dawes Bill which was approved February 8, 1887, provided that equal quantities of land be allowed the Shawnees and Pottawatomies. This helped somewhat, as it removed that source of Shawnee resentment. In this their second allotment, each head of a family received one hundred and sixty acres of agricultural land, or double that of grazing land; to each person of eighteen years or over, not married, and to each orphan regardless of age eighty acres of agricultural land, or double that quantity of grazing land; to each child under eighteen years old, forty acres of agricultural, or double that quantity of grazing land was allotted. The married women received no allotment unless they demanded it, then they were assigned half the land allowed the head of the family.

Those of our people who had originally accepted their allotments under the leadership of Chief Joe Ellis or John Sparney (White Turkey was now the chief) readily accepted their additional allotments, but those under Big Jim and Sam Warrior stood firm in their resistance until the last. They even refused to give their names so that a census or allotment roll could be made out, and there was much trouble and unpleasantness. Even the U. S. Indian police failed to secure their names, and we were in despair about gaining our point.

Finally I thought out a plan that worked pretty well, although for a time even that seemed about to fail. One of my pupils, a girl named Ellen Bullfrog, whose family I have already mentioned, was a very intelligent girl and I enlisted her sympathy and help in my difficulty.

My plan was that Ellen should go among the people of Big Jim's band, as she usually did, to their dances and other social gatherings, and to visit in their homes. Thus she was to learn the names of all the heads of families and their children, their age, sex, and relationship. She wrote these down secretly, and turned the list over to me, and from them I compiled the roll. Of them all she made only two mistakes; in one case she assigned the male sex to a female child, and in the other she listed the pet name of a child that already had been enrolled under its right name. Thus we succeeded in compiling a roll of the Absentee Shawnee tribe of Indians which stands today, proven to be correct, and was accepted by the U. S. Indian office. Ellen was well paid for her work—but it was kept a secret for many years.

Major N. S. Porter of Nebraska, a special agent of the government, had charge of the allotment of land to our people. He was a man I admired very much, a successful farmer in his own state, and a good judge of land. He was patient and sympathetic with the bewildered Indians. He knew that farming must be their chief occupation, and he proved himself a true friend by advising them which land to select.

I applied to him for a position on his staff, and he gladly took me on. When I commenced work with the surveying party I was given the place of axman, but was soon promoted to flagman, then chainman, and finally I was made surveyor. All that time I was acting as interpreter, and trying to explain everything to the Indians, trying to reconcile them to the inevitable change that was coming to us all. Working with the white men, I could more easily explain just what they were going to do.

With my assistants I was assigned to do the surveying of the land allotted to Big Jim and his band of followers. They were in a sullen mood, and notwithstanding our relationship and the confidence he had in my integrity, my uncle would not listen to my reasoning or explanations. He and his followers resisted our intrusion and pulled up my corner stakes as fast as I could establish them.

But in spite of Big Jim's resistance the great work finally was finished with individual allotments as provided by the Dawes Bill. I hardly realized at that time the great significance it had for my people. The Absentee Shawnee Indians were the first Indians who had land offered them by the government, thus making them citizens of the United States. The others did not comprehend it and showed no appreciation of the fact. Neither did they accept the citizenship, but kept up their tribal system, as if nothing could change that.

A LITTLE DIVERSION

XXI

DURING those strenuous, stormy years when my time was divided between work for the United States Government and work for my own people, our home life had gone smoothly along. My lovely young wife had done her full share in the home-making and had shown a keen sympathy and interest in my work.

Three little boys, Pierre, Paul, and Reece, had come to gladden our hearts and make our home complete. We had added many comforts to our house, as the years passed, and we had many friends among the missionaries and teachers, who visited us occasionally. Although we lived far from a railroad or a large town, we were near one of the great cattle trails which was used for general travel and many travelers found their way to our door, thus bringing news and gossip of the world that we otherwise would not have heard. With so many white people coming into the country, one way or another, we had mails more regularly, and many little expressions of interest came to us from the great world east of us. We each had our regular correspondents whose letters brought us news of the doings of our friends. We subscribed to papers and magazines that told of things that were interesting in the world of science and literature, while once in a great while some friend or relative would come to pay us a pleasant visit.

One visit I remember especially because of the pleasure it seemed to give our guests, as well as ourselves. It was soon after I had resigned my position in the boarding school that we received a letter from Arkansas City, Kansas, signed by Joe White, a boy my wife had known in Tennessee, saying that he and a friend of his, William Jenkins, another young fellow, wanted to come to make us a visit, and incidentally do a little hunting—having heard so many stories about hunting trips in the Indian Territory.

I invited them to come, and a few days later they arrived. After a few days of visiting we prepared for a camping trip, and the boys and I set out for the Little River country which abounded in game, such as deer, turkeys, quail, and ducks. I soon became acquainted with the boys who were at the age when they most enjoy outdoor life and hunting, and were keen for experience in a wild country, such as they believed this to be.

It was a great adventure for the boys, and after the day's hunt we would sit about a campfire and talk together. They never tired of asking me questions nor of listening to the stories I could tell them. And in turn they told me many things that were interesting to me. They especially liked to have me tell them about the habits and peculiarities of wild creatures.

One evening we were sitting before the campfire, talking thus, and they had me tell them in my own tongue the different things that birds and animals do. As for instance, the horse neighs, the mule brays, the dog barks, the turkey gobbles, the grouse drums, the duck—what did the duck do? For the life of us, we could not think what was peculiar to the duck. Then we decided with a great shout of laughter that "a drake drakes." The fun they had about that simple thing was indicative of their youth and innocence. From that time on "a drake drakes" became the phrase of recognition in our camp. If any one of us happened to be out late, or if we met in the darkness, one would naturally call out,

"Who comes here?" And instantly the answer would be, "A drake drakes."

After several happy weeks the boys returned to their home in Kansas, but in the correspondence we kept up for some time, always there was some reference to "a drake drakes."

I never have seen Joe White since, but have heard that he was a successful business man of El Reno, Oklahoma, where he was postmaster in the early days. The following note which I received from him soon after his return shows an interesting glimpse of the rapid progress made in the development of Arkansas City about that time.

Arkansas City, Kansas
December 11, 1887

Mr. Thomas W. Alford,
Dear Friend:

In writing to you before, I forgot to mention the dried corn which you offered to give me. Suppose you could send me a peck? Also if you could dig up a ham of venison, I should like it very much.

Arkansas City is on a great building boom. The railroad has been completed to this place, and trains now are coming regularly. The canal is to be enlarged at once. Electric lights started last night. The gas works have been completed, and such things make a lively town.

I often think of our hunting trip with pleasure. Wonder if coyotes have caught the turkey I wounded yet? And do the "drakes drake"? I'll remember that as long as I live.

Wm. Jenkens sends regards to yourself and wife. Hoping to hear from you soon, I remain,

Your friend,
Joe White

THE OPENING OF OKLAHOMA

XXII

AFTER the work of preparing the roll and surveying allotments for the Shawnees was completed I undertook some work for the Sac and Fox Indian Agent and was sent with a party of teamsters to haul freight from what was then Oklahoma Station on the Santa Fe railroad. I had under my charge ten Shawnee men with wagons and teams.

It was in April, 1889, just before the original opening of Oklahoma Territory for homestead entry. We arrived at the west boundary of the Pottawatomie-Shawnee reservation about noon one day, and found the boundary line which was plainly marked, lined with campers. There were a great many with loaded wagons, some on horseback—all camping and waiting for the fateful day and hour when the country would be declared open for settlement. They seemed to represent all classes of people and presented a strange and interesting sight to the Indian men with me, as perhaps we did to them.

Some of the people tried to talk to us, and asked us questions about the country. Probably many of them were afraid of us, especially the women and children, for some of them looked at us with very wide open eyes and breathless interest.

Some of the men told me that we would not be allowed to cross the line into Oklahoma Territory, but I knew that as our errand was for an agent of the government we would be allowed to go, so I took my men on across the

[142]

line. We camped that night near Wantlan's ranch, on Concho Creek.

The next morning we went on towards Oklahoma Station. We met some soldiers who told me that we could not get our freight that day, so we camped at the bend of the North Canadian River, where later a brickyard was established, and which now is a part of Oklahoma City.

We remained there during the day of the opening of Oklahoma and witnessed one of the most spectacular events in the history of this western country. I have no doubt there are men and women in Oklahoma today, who remember the group of Indians camped at the bend of the river on the day of the opening. We had nothing to do but wait for the great event, and all of the men were curious to see how the paleface took his allotment.

This opening was that of the part of Indian Territory known as the "Oklahoma Land," and a short sketch of its history might be appropriate in this place. The term Oklahoma Land was applied to a strip of land in the Indian Territory that had never been assigned to any tribe of Indians, and on which there was no Indian reservation. Some railroad attorney, trying to secure a right of way for his road through the Indian Territory (which was bitterly opposed by the Indians), had made the discovery that this small body of land was unassigned and unclaimed. His report had raised the question as to whether it was available for homestead entry under the laws of the country pertaining to free homes.

Immediately there was a great excitement about Oklahoma Land, which was conceded to be of great value. In fact so great was the agitation that the newspapers were full of it for many months. There was a strong sentiment prevalent that this land should be available for white people's homes, and settlers were continually coming over the Kansas line and staking their claims. The U. S. troops were kept busy ejecting such people by force.

For ten years this question was left unsettled. Every Congress had the matter up for discussion. Some politicians wanted the land opened for white settlers, while others contended that it belonged to the Indians and should be reserved for their use.

On March 2, 1889, the last day of the Fiftieth Congress, the essential features of the bill providing for the opening of the country were inserted into a clause of the Indian Appropriations Bill as an amendment, and thus passed both houses, unnoticed by the opponents of the measure. Three weeks after the passage of the bill, President Harrison issued a proclamation which opened the unassigned Oklahoma Land to white citizens of the United States for homestead entry.

I think I may truthfully say that there are comparatively few people living in this great state today who are familiar with the conditions under which this great commonwealth became a "white man's country." Subsequent openings of Indian Territory for white settlement was upon Indian land held as reservations. When they were opened for white homesteaders, as I shall describe later on, it was after the government had allotted a homestead or a certain number of acres to each member of the tribe and bought the remainder of the reservation from the tribe to which it belonged. White men were allowed to take up the unallotted land as homesteads. The money paid for the land was divided so that each member of the tribe received his share.

As much as I then knew about the opening of the new country, I explained to the men with me, as we patiently waited for the rush to begin.

The time set for the opening was to be at noon, when soldiers at Oklahoma Station were to fire pistols as a signal for the rush to start. Any person who crossed the line before the signal was fired took an undue advantage, and forfeited his right to file on the land.

As we were camped several miles beyond the border line we were surprised to see two individuals on horseback, a young man and a young woman, emerge from the brush before noon. They came towards us at a gallop and passed, racing towards a point northeast of us. When about a quarter of a mile from us we saw the young woman jump from her horse and stick a stake in the ground, thus claiming the homestead right to that quarter-section. The man went on farther and placed his stake. He rode a fine sorrel horse and the woman rode a gray.

My men wanted to know what they were doing. I told them I did not know, unless they were taking their allotments, which I knew they were not entitled to do at that time. We learned afterward that a protest was made against the claims of the young couple who raced past us. The contest was in the courts for several years, and a party of Indians who were camped at the bend of the river were wanted for witnesses, but we did not want to be mixed up in any legal affairs, so we kept quiet about it, and I do not know how the suit terminated.

About one o'clock in the afternoon prospective settlers from the eastern line began to arrive on horseback, their horses panting and covered with sweat. They were followed later by people in wagons, buggies, and carts, in fact every description of vehicle that would haul goods or people—all filled with anxious, eager home-seekers.

Later in the afternoon the first train arrived from the south, and it was *loaded*. Every inch of space in the cars was filled with human beings of all descriptions. All carried some luggage. Some had an ax, or a spade, or a gun; all carried some kind of a satchel which no doubt held their clothing. The very tops of the cars were crowded with human beings, some even clinging to the sides of the cars, and hanging on to the platforms.

Before the train came to a full stop the people began to swarm out in a mad mass, running wildly in every direction. Some were yelling at the top of their voices for horses to ride. Some were shouting to their comrades or in contest over their claims, women screeched and screamed, men swore loudly as they ran, stumbling, falling, only to get up and rush like mad again, trying to outrun some opponent. In fact the din was so great that it would have put an Indian war whoop to shame.

Some of the people were satisfied with staking city lots, while others wanted to go into the country. As there were no horses or teams to be hired many set out in a run for the country. Seeing our teams, some ran to us, and soon there was a mob surrounding our camp, pleading breathlessly to be taken into the country, offering us money, their coats, anything they had, if only we would take them out where they might stake their claims.

I told the men they might take them out, for we could not get our freight that day anyway. So the people crowded into the wagons, and the men took them out, in different directions, and later returned, well paid and very much amused at the eagerness of the white man to secure a homestead.

That night Oklahoma City was a city of white tents. Stores were opened with barely a handful of goods, lawyers had tacked up their signs, doctors had set up for practice. Zealous churchmen had staked locations for churches, and the business of living had been started in the town. All kinds of food and even water were being sold at ridiculously high prices. Thus began the settlement of Oklahoma City, long to be remembered by those fortunate enough to have had a part in it.

It was indeed a strange sight to my teamsters, for they saw how eager the white man was to secure his allotment from the government, and perhaps they returned home with a little more appreciation of our own situation.

When we were able to load our freight from the depot we started home, and all along the way until we crossed the Oklahoma line we saw people, the new settlers busy with their home-making. The camp where we had spent the night before we reached Oklahoma Station was in possession of a settler. Some people had tents, some had cut brush and made arbors under which they could live, others were digging for dear life to make a "dugout" which was a popular form of abode at that time. The dugout was made by digging a large cave or cellar in the side of a hill, with heavy timbers across the top, on which sod was piled in such a fashion as to keep the room dry and clean. Some people lined the walls of their dugouts with rocks, and really they made very comfortable homes, or were considered so at that time.

To witness this opening was a great experience to me, as well as to the men who were with me. It gave me a new conception of the ways of the white man, and his character. In fact, it is hard for me to realize that some of the distinguished-looking, dignified people I meet as I go about Oklahoma City or other parts of the state, are some of those same wild-looking, shoving, grasping, shouting individuals we saw that day when Oklahoma was opened. It makes me wonder too, if civilized people could not learn something from their Indian brothers—self-control?

INDIANS AT COURT

XXIII

ALTHOUGH it was about twenty miles from the Shawnee reservation to the Oklahoma line, or to Oklahoma City proper, the advent of so many white people with their business enterprise, their energetic, vigorous way of doing things had a very noticeable effect on our people. So many of our younger ones could speak English—thanks to the government school—that in almost every family there was someone who could interpret, and it was easier to trade with the white people. We no longer depended entirely upon the licensed trader for our commodities. More markets and the proximity of shipping points brought better prices for our cattle or whatever we had to sell or trade.

But there were disadvantages too. Always a crowd of gamblers and adventurers follow in the wake of a new settlement, and to a certain extent we were at their mercy. We knew very little about the laws or the courts of the white man, and from our early training we were suspicious of them, never realizing that they might afford us protection or security in our rights. But we soon had a very real experience with courts, when we were involved in a notable case tried before Judge Henry W. Scott, in Oklahoma City. The defendants in the case were Thomas Washington (better known as Long Tom), Blue Coat, and Switch Little Ax, who were charged with the murder of three white men.

Several months before the killing for which these men were tried some Negroes had been stealing horses from the

[148]

Shawnees. Once the thieves had been trailed into the rough country in the southeastern part of the territory, and after a fight, the horses were recovered. A few weeks later Long Tom heard a commotion among his horses one night, and sent his son and Charley Switch (son of Switch Little Ax) to investigate the cause of the disturbance. It was early in the night, but quite dark. Charley soon returned, and reported that he had found three men rounding up the horses. He had yelled at them and also shot his gun in their direction. Long Tom and the boys then went down and drove the horses into the corral for the night. They believed the would-be thieves were the three Negroes who had been giving others so much trouble.

The next morning the three men, Long Tom, Blue Coat, and Switch Little Ax got on their horses and trailed the thieves. They had no difficulty in finding the trail, and followed it for several miles before it turned north. They found where the thieves had crossed the river, and in the sand they found a little pool of blood, which was evidence that Charley had hit one of them when he fired at them the night before. The trail continued, north and east, into a deep ravine covered with timber, where they discovered the men camping. The Indians got off their horses but were discovered by the men, who assisted their wounded companion to his horse. They mounted their horses and fired upon Long Tom and his companions as they galloped away.

The Indians took to the trees and returned the fire. As the fugitives reached higher and more open ground they were picked from their horses by the Indians as they would have shot deer on the run. When the Indians reached the place where the fugitives lay, they all were dead, except one, who was dying, and as Long Tom told in court he shot the man, "to put him out of his misery." But to the surprise of the Indians they found that the men they had

killed were not their Negro enemies, but white men. So
Long Tom left his companions to watch, telling them not
to touch the men or anything belonging to them, and he
rode to the Sauk and Fox Agency and reported the deed.

Lee Patrick, then commissioner at the Agency, returned
with Long Tom and took charge of the dead and their
property. Later the men were tried before Lee Patrick
and discharged, and they believed the matter closed.

But in the following term of court at Oklahoma City,
relatives of the dead men went before the grand jury and had
the Indians indicted. They were released on bond, however, because all the property found on the dead men was
proven to be property stolen from farmers in the western
part of Oklahoma.

The case was continued from one term of court to another
for two years. In the meantime the defendants had engaged
a lawyer, but he left the country immediately after col-
lecting his retainer fee and refused to return unless additional fees were paid him. This they refused to do, and just
before the trial they engaged the firm of Lewis and Reddick
to defend them. United States Assistant Attorney John F.
Stone conducted the prosecution. He was an able man.

I felt that a great responsibility was being imposed upon
me when I was sworn to translate the Shawnee language
into English, and the English into Shawnee for the defendants. I was struck with awe at the solemnity of the
court and the demeanor of those connected with it. It all
was new to me.

The defendants sat quietly, with the same dignified
demeanor that was their custom when a crisis was at hand.
In the trial that followed they answered questions simply
and related all that led up to the tragedy as above stated,
denying nothing. They admitted killing the men, even to
the last shot of Long Tom's to ease the dying man. The trial

[150]

was long drawn out and our suspense was terrible, but the Indians maintained their quiet, dignified composure throughout all the complex procedure.

It was late in the evening when the case finally was turned over to the jury, and there was a great uneasiness upon us. Our attorneys seemed unusually grave, which we thought meant resignation to an unfavorable verdict. Long Tom handed his pocketbook to me, with some instructions regarding his affairs, and the other two defendants did the same. No doubt they expected an immediate execution if they were convicted.

While the jury deliberated, one of the attorneys told me that the jury was made up mostly of farmers who suffered most from horse thieves. He had confidence that they would render a favorable verdict. I did not repeat what he said to the defendants, because I did not want to give them false hopes. The courtroom was packed with people, many of them farmers who seemed to be as much interested as we were.

It was near midnight when the jury filed in, and one of them handed a paper to the judge, who read it without a change of countenance, then handed it to the clerk of the court. Absolute silence reigned in the courtroom, as the people sat tense, waiting for the clerk to read the fateful words. The clerk rose and read the verdict to the defendants, who sat unmoved in their seats, until I had translated the last phrase, "not guilty."

Then Blue Coat and Switch Little Ax rose, with every eye upon them, walked briskly across the room and shook hands with every one of the jurymen, then returned to their seats.

Long Tom remained seated, and never changed countenance, as became one of his race. The judge gave them all a short lecture to the effect that they must not take the law into their own hands, but allow the officers to do that. When I had interpreted that, Long Tom made a quick motion to me. "Tell the judge for me," he said, "that if any man comes to round up my horses before my eyes, shall I allow him to take them? No. I will do the same thing again."

I hesitated to interpret this to the judge, but he saved me with the question, "What did he say?"

I repeated in English what Long Tom had said, and again there was a commotion of approval in the courtroom. I think everyone in the courtroom came and shook hands with us, even to the judge himself. That ended my experience with the courts for a while.

Many years later, Mrs. Harry B. Gilstrap, sister of Lee Patrick mentioned as the commissioner before whom these men first were tried, told of the bringing in of the bodies of the thieves to the Agency.

"I was standing in the door at the Agency when some Indians drove a wagon into the yard. There was something covered up in the wagon. The men went around to the back of the wagon, and pulled out a huge bundle wrapped in a wagon sheet. The bundle evidently was too heavy for they could not carry it and it fell to the ground. Imagine how I felt when the bodies of three dead white men rolled out of that sheet." After a moment Mrs. Gilstrap went on. "My brother Lee had sent the Indians to bring in the bodies, for he had to go to Oklahoma City to report their death. He forgot that I was alone that day at the Agency."

OUR RESERVATION IS OPENED

XXIV

IN 1891 I was appointed as surveyor for the government under William Walker of Oklahoma City, a special agent for the purpose of allotting the Sauk and Fox lands. We began our work near the agency, and from there moved our camp to a place near the home of Henry Jones, an interpreter for many years for the Sauk and Fox Indians. We worked down the river, to where the Shawnee Clubhouse now stands.

I had to give up that work however, after about a month's time, to be at home with my wife, whose health and strength seemed to be failing rapidly. While taking care of her, doing all that I could for her comfort, I still had time to care for my cattle, having accumulated about seventy-five head. It was comparatively easy to raise cattle in those days, for we had a free range, and the sale of a steer helped materially with the ever increasing living expenses. Having an abundance of milk, cream, and butter for all purposes added greatly to the delight of our table.

That was the year that the Pottawatomie-Shawnee reservation was opened for white settlement, and a memorable one in many respects. Stories of the great value of the land had gone out over the whole United States, and a great many people were determined to get homesteads in the new country. The opening of the Oklahoma country in 1889 had been so successful that many had regretted not having tried to participate in that opening. Even those skeptical ones who had doubted the value of the new land or the wisdom of starting out in a new country were now anxious to try their luck. Others who had feared "an Indian uprising or massacre" had laid aside their fears and were eager to exercise their homestead rights, and there are always a great many people who are anxious to get anything the government is giving away. The homesteads were not being given away, but the terms of payment were so lenient that everyone thought he would be able to meet them when they came due. Many, no doubt, trusted that a free homes bill would be passed in the course of time. At any rate there were a great many people who wanted homesteads in the country to be opened.

It was a tempestuous year. Parties of "Sooners," people trying to get located before the regular opening, were continually prowling about, ready to take any advantage that could be devised. Companies of soldiers and government officials were kept constantly on the defensive. The Shawnees, especially those under the leadership of Big Jim and Sam Warrior, were still unreconciled to the opening of their country, and maintained a sullen and offensive attitude towards all white people who came into the country. I did what I could, counseled my people and explained to them the advantages that were likely to come to us from the opening. But my voice could scarcely be heard above the strong voice of dissensions and discontent.

Having witnessed the "run" at the opening of Oklahoma, I determined to take a chance myself when Tecumseh, the county seat town of County B (now Pottawatomie County) was opened. I was told that I would not be allowed to hold the lots if I did stake them, but I thought the fun would be worth the trouble. Hence, when a line was formed surrounding the site laid out for the county seat on September 22, 1891, I was in place with the others, eager for the adventure.

Among the many amusing and interesting events of that day was the fact that a huge buck deer was surrounded on the townsite, which was one mile square. Being unable to pass the line of would-be citizens the frightened animal kept running from side to side in its efforts to escape. No one dared to shoot for fear of hitting someone inside the line or on the opposite line. But when the officer in command fired the gun which gave the signal for the run, in the turmoil and confusion that ensued no further thought was given to the deer, and I do not know what finally became of him.

I was successful in obtaining two lots on the north side of the county seat and soon became acquainted with those people whose lots adjoined mine, and we were able to assist each other as witnesses in the filing of claims. I obtained title to my lots without question, and later sold them for a reasonable profit.

The following month (October 27, 1891, to be exact), I was appointed surveyor of the county by George W. Steele, then governor of Oklahoma Territory. This gave me my first chance to serve my white fellow citizens, in settling boundary lines of claims, and in opening up roads to markets.

Committees were appointed in adjacent counties to open roads between the county seats. Each road was to start at the county seat and meet somewhere on the county line. Our committee started at once on their line west, which is the present highway to Norman, in Cleveland County, where it connects with other roads, branching out into a system of highways that reaches to the uttermost parts of our nation. Norman later was selected as the site of our state university.

Our side of the line was timbered, and the landmarks were easily found, so it was comparatively easy to survey. On the Cleveland County side of the line the land is a rolling prairie, and landmarks were obscure. Therefore we soon passed the western boundary of our county and met somewhere in Cleveland County.

The Cleveland County committee was headed by Mr. W. C. Renfrow, who later became governor of Oklahoma. While our boys were getting dinner on the day we met the Cleveland County delegation, Mr. Renfrow asked me to return with him on the line he had passed to locate some marks that he had failed to get accurately. Leaving my instrument, which we thought we would not need, we soon lost the trail. The farther we went the more puzzled we became as to directions. We tried to return to our party, but that was impossible, and we decided it was the boys we had left preparing dinner who were lost. The sky was heavy with clouds and the day bitterly cold. We wandered about, hungry and cold, and my Indian instinct as to direction seemed to have left me.

Finally we saw something in the distance that looked like a mound thrown up by a dugout. We hurried to the place and found a middle-aged woman the only occupant of the lonely place, which after all was a rather comfortable one-room abode.

We asked the woman about directions, and she told us where she had seen the surveyors at work. As it was far past noon we asked if she could give us something to eat. She cooked some bacon and eggs and made us some coffee, all the food her meager larder contained, for even then her husband had gone to town to buy groceries.

Refreshed and warmed, we soon found our way back to the camp where the boys joked us heartily about being lost.

Notwithstanding my education, my connection with the missionaries, and even my marriage to a white woman, I was unfamiliar with the ways of white people. I knew absolutely nothing about politics and the machinery that works behind all forms of government. My learning has been slow and painful. (It is still in a state of infancy, I am afraid.) Although my own people looked upon white men with distrust, my education had taught me to trust them, hence I could not understand the difference that politics seemed to make in gentlemanly conduct any more than I could see the difference in religion and denominationalism. These are mysteries beyond me.

I was drafted into the Republican party by my appointment as county surveyor by the governor. At the expiration of my appointment I became a candidate for re-election on the Republican ticket. I was defeated by my Democratic opponent by a few votes, which ended my political activity in the county.

While all these events were taking place I was living with my family on our home place, the Bird's Nest. We attended the Friends' church at the mission, in which I served as clerk of the meetings for many years. I did not fully agree with the Friends' doctrine of nonresistance. I had been taught by my father and by my teachers at Hampton that it was the duty of every citizen to defend his loved ones and his country and to die if necessary in this defense. Even wild creatures defend their young, but these holy people taught a different doctrine.

Another thing; I was taught while in school to avoid the superstitions of my people, and I was convinced that it was the thing to do when I came back among them. For instance, I had been told by my own ancestors of the earthquake that Tecumseh predicted when he visited the Creek Indians for the last time and tried to get them to join his

[157]

confederacy against the white people. When he left them he told them that when he returned to a certain place (the vicinity of the present city of Detroit, Michigan), he would stamp his foot on the ground and the earth would tremble, and it would shake down all the houses in the town. It is a matter of history that the earthquake did occur and every one of their houses was shaken to the ground. This is a superstition to the white people, and I believe with them. But why is a miracle predicted by an Indian a superstition, while that by a white man or a Jew is not a superstition but a prophecy? From the viewpoint of either—though the color of their skin is different—each saw the miracle for the good of his race. I am unable to answer this question, and I believe no one else can and be reasonable. I hope that the time will come when man will know more about God's laws, which we call natural laws. When that time comes we will know more about so-called miracles and marvels attributed to the prophets.

During those years that my wife and I attended the little mission church I had a class in Sabbath school. I tried to teach the beauties and importance of the life of our Savior, Jesus Christ, as contained in His Gospels, but I avoided discussion of the miracles, because I could not teach what I did not understand myself.

During the year of 1892 my wife's health was bad. Except for my little excursion into politics which I have related I was kept rather closely at home, helping her with the housekeeping and trying to make what I believed to be her last days as comfortable and pleasant as possible. Yet I maintained a keen interest in all that was going on about me—the development of a wild country by the white man.

THE UNITED STATES INDIAN SERVICE

XXV

MY WIFE'S health continued to fail rapidly, until December 22, 1892, when she went to her final reward, leaving me with our three little boys in the "nest" we had planned and built together. With the "Mother Bird" gone the nest had lost its charm and was to us a place of desolation.

The Friends' mission to the Kickapoos was located about two miles north of the present city of McLoud, and I had some very good friends there and often attended their service. Among them was Sister Elizabeth Test, one of the most devout members of the congregation. I was fortunate in being able to make arrangements with her to take care of my little boys and to begin their education.

Early in the next year, 1893, I again entered the Indian service as a teacher of farming to the Kickapoos, under Samuel L. Patrick, U. S. Indian Agent, who was the father of Lee Patrick, whom I have mentioned before. Both of these men were of high moral character and gave their very best efforts to the welfare of those under their charge.

Soon after that however, at the urgent advice of my friends I applied for an appointment as special Indian agent to have charge of the allotting of land to the Kickapoos. Having had some experience with the allotment of land to our own people, I felt that I might be of material benefit to the Kickapoos in helping them select their future homes. I was thoroughly familiar with the land that was to be divided, and I had some knowledge of farming. The Indians knew very little about farming and did not know the value of the land and in many instances were bitterly opposed to the allotment. They certainly were at a great disadvantage when given an opportunity to select their homesites. This seemed to me to be another chance to serve my race, if not my own tribe. As I have said I applied for the appointment. The written recommendation from all the county officers, and from Reverend Charles W. Kirk, who then was superintendent of the Friends' Mission, and others who were interested in me, I still treasure.

But instead of my getting the appointment it was given to my friend, Major Moses Neal, and he at once offered me the position of surveyor of the allotments, which I accepted. Being on friendly terms with the Kickapoos and acting as their interpreter, I still was able to give them some advice about selecting their homes.

This work continued through the winter and spring, and until June of 1894 when allotments were completed, and again I was without a job. Some time during that year General Edward L. Thomas succeeded Major Samuel Patrick as U. S. Indian Agent at the Sauk and Fox Agency. (The Shawnees, Kickapoos, Pottawatomies, and Iowas still were under that agency at that time.)

As I look back upon that time it seems that it might be called a period of reconstruction, for it was just after the passing of an act of Congress which abolished tribal government, and all of the different tribes of Indians were under United States laws, and were to be governed and dealt with by the same. It was hard for the agencies to handle situations that arose continually, and the Indians were restless and unhappy, resenting the invasion of the white people and denying the right of the government to take their lands and force them to give up their own government and abide by laws they did not understand.

It was on the thirteenth day of September, 1893 that Agent Thomas informed the Shawnees that he had been directed by the Commissioner of Indian Affairs to submit for approval the names of seven of the most prominent men of the tribe who would constitute a Business Committee to supercede the chiefs and councilors of the old tribal government. The Business Committee was to represent the Absentee Shawnees as a tribe in all dealings with the United States and to act in an advisory capacity to the individual members of the tribe. They were to certify to the identity of grantors of sales of land and to act for the tribe in other matters.

A few days later I was informed by letter that the following names had been forwarded as members of the Business Committee: Thomas W. Alford, Thomas Washington (Long Tom), John C. King, John Welch, Switch Little Ax, and the two chiefs, White Turkey and Big Jim. As my name was first on the list, I was made chairman automatically and was in reality at last in the position of chief or principal adviser of my people, recognized as such by the government at Washington.

After the list had been approved by the Commissioner of Indian Affairs, Big Jim and John Welch refused to serve, and Thomas Rock and Walter Shawnee were substituted. At the first meeting of the committee I was chosen by its members as chairman, and Walter Shawnee as secretary. This office I still hold, for the committee still is in existence, but its members have dropped out, by death, or removed from cause, until now I alone of the original seven remain. How long will the committee last? I cannot say. That is with the government which caused its appointment. The Secretary of the Interior has already taken away the object for which it came into existence, by taking upon that office the duties first assigned to the Business Committee. It could be of great benefit to the Shawnee people in many ways, but that is in the hands of the government where it originated. As a matter of fact many otherwise intelligent agents prefer to deal with the Indians through the old tribal system of recognition, to the detriment of the younger generation every year attaining manhood. The Dawes Commission long ago abolished this practice in favor of good citizenship, a fact that these agents are disposed to ignore.

The Committee had a great deal of trouble in the beginning of its existence. Unscrupulous persons were continually trying to take advantage of the ignorance or credulity of the Indians. There was much illegal leasing of land for farming purposes; leases often were obtained running from five to twenty years with little or insufficient consideration. There were people who tried and sometimes were successful in inserting clauses in the Indian appropriations bills of Congress that were greatly adverse to the interests of the Indians.

These matters always received our attention when brought to our notice, and in many instances we were able to protect the interests of our people, though not always. However, I can truthfully say that the Business Committee has tried to the best of its ability to assist the United States Indian agents. The members never have received a salary or any pay for their service, except an occasional small fee for signing a grantor's certificate.

It would be hard to describe the change that had come over the country since it had opened for white settlement, but one must keep that change in mind to understand the situation of the Indians and to understand just how they were affected by the succeeding periods of development. It is true that no other history of pioneering is like the opening of this country for white settlement. There was no precedent in the dramatic dawning of a new era in the country. No other country was ever so quickly settled, or with so cosmopolitan a population as Oklahoma. Our own reservation was just as spectacular.

Tecumseh, the county seat of the new county, the opening of which I have already mentioned, was a thriving little city within three months after it was opened, and there was no railroad or waterway to bring supplies into the country. There were not even good roads to the nearest freight depots. But such roads as we had were filled with wagons and buggies and hacks, hauling supplies and building material and people into the new town. Business houses, homes, churches, were springing up like the proverbial mushrooms. All this was startling and appalling to the Shawnees.

Then like a meteoric flash came the news that a railroad was to be built through the country. To the white settlers this was joyous news, but to our people it brought only more wonder and regret, more assurance that they would be pushed and crowded, more fear that they eventually would have to give up what homes they had, and "move on."

The railroad was to have come through Tecumseh. There were those who claimed that they were cheated out of the road, others said it was simply a matter of graft—that people who wanted to boost Shawnee paid a large sum of money to have the road routed away from Tecumseh and through Shawnee. I do not know the real cause, but when the final survey was completed the road did not come through Tecumseh by five miles, and the Shawnee townsite was platted. I located the original corners, little dreaming that I ever would see such a city as the one that stands there now, one of the most substantial of our great commonwealth.

[163]

The vigorous fight between the two new towns must have served as an advertisement, for by the time the new railroad was running through the country the little village of Shawnee was overrun with people. This was a wonderful cotton growing country, and the people who had taken up homesteads planted most of their land in the snowy staple. With the railroad going through, Shawnee became a shipping point for a radius of thirty miles or more. In fact Shawnee became the best cotton market in the country.

There was the usual crowd of gamblers and vile humanity that flock to all new towns; to some of these the Indians were easy prey. It kept the Business Committee vigilant and busy protecting their interests. Saloons were open in both Tecumseh and Shawnee, and the Indians often gave way to their old weakness and drank too much liquor.

There was a story told about the people of Tecumseh and the surrounding community that afforded a great deal of amusement to the Indians. It was soon after the new courthouse was built when some lawless and troublesome members of the Seminole tribe who lived near the eastern border of our county, would cross over into the county and give offense to the white people settled there. They were arrogant and threatening, and really did give a great deal of trouble. The white people resented the intrusion and I believe an Indian was killed. However I am not sure about that.

But a rumor got spread about that there was to be an "Indian uprising." To most of the people in the little town an Indian was simply an Indian, and they knew absolutely nothing about the different tribes, or their dispositions. The rumor that the Indians were on the warpath grew, until finally the white people became thoroughly frightened, most of them believing that all the Indians in the country would join together and invade the town, burning the houses of the people as they came.

Runners were sent to warn friends living in the country and late in the day a crowd gathered at the courthouse. The people brought their belongings, bedding, clothing, and even groceries. The women and children spent the night in the courthouse, while the men patrolled the streets fully armed, and all expecting trouble. But no Indians appeared and the people lost their fears and returned peacefully to their homes.

I remember that a white woman who lived near us came to our house that night thinking that we at least were friendly, and asked for our protection. I laughed at her and told her that I too was an Indian but she did not seem to be afraid of me. Old settlers of Tecumseh and the surrounding country still laugh about that experience.

With all this booming and building of the new country among the white people there was not much prosperity for us. Several months passed when I had no work, and had difficulty paying for the care of my little boys. Although I was a pretty good workman at several different kinds of labor, no one seemed to want to hire an Indian, when there were white men to do the work.

When the railroad was built through the country the town of McLoud was started near the Kickapoo Mission, and as I was interpreter for the Friends' Sunday service there the railroad kindly gave me a pass to McLoud. I thus was able to spend some time each week with my boys, which was a great pleasure to them and to me. We often took long rambles in the woods together or in winter we sat before the fire and talked. We were very congenial companions and did not like to be separated.

About this time a very kind lady from Kansas City visited the Friends' Mission at McLoud and became interested in my little boys. She asked me to let her take them home with her for a visit. I gave my consent and she kept them for more than a year, sending them to school, and giving them much better advantages than they could have had at the crowded mission school, for which she has our everlasting gratitude. I missed the children very badly, but did not give up my visits to the Kickapoo Mission, for I had some very good friends there. One of the teachers had been especially kind to my little boys and we had many other interests in common. Sister Test encouraged my visits and I continued to act as interpreter.

I record all this because it will explain why I had so much acquaintance with the Kickapoos. They realized that I was their friend and had confidence in me. Because of that I was able to be of some benefit to them a few years later, as I shall relate in the proper place.

In 1896 I again entered the Indian service for a short time as clerk and interpreter for John T. Oglesby, a special agent in making farm leases and for legalizing those found to be just and canceling those found fraudulent. Mr. Oglesby had headquarters in Shawnee for several months, but in June of 1897 his work was turned over to the Sauk and Fox Agency, and again I was out of work.

During the years that I have told about I gave a great deal of my attention to the translation of the Gospel of Jesus Christ into the Shawnee language, a work that I had begun while teaching school. The more that I read and studied the English language, the more my admiration grew for my own Shawnee language, and I was anxious to preserve it in all its purity and beauty. In the description of nature and things natural, and in the idea of things intangible, the inner man, the soul, the Spirit and God, the Shawnee language is peculiarly sweet and full, and seems to stand alone. I debated a long time in what manner it was best to try to preserve the

[166]

language and fell to the thought that the Gospels will live always, hence that would be the best method of preserving my own native tongue. I translated first the old version, but later changed and revised my work in accordance with the revised version.[1]

There never was any prospect of material reward for this work, which has taken many long, tedious hours of hard mental labor; nothing save the joy and satisfaction of accomplishing my object. I fully realize that under our present system of commercialism, this would be called foolishness, and the idea of obtaining joy and satisfaction in saving a language that otherwise would be forgotten is likely to be called egotism or selfishness. Be it so. My people were among those who once owned this vast country, they were strong and brave and virtuous, according to their knowledge. If they have failed to live up to the standards of the white race, they at least have fought for their own convictions. Who can say that in future generations they will not contribute something of untold value to the life of our nation? Surely strength of character is a commendable trait and our white friends would very well profit by some of our tribal teachings, such as loyalty, perseverance, and self-reliance. Perhaps future generations will want some knowledge of these people—will search to find their natural tongue. Anyway the Shawnee language is full of majesty and sweetness, and I have done all that I could to preserve it in its purity and beauty.

1. *The Four Gospels of our Lord Jesus Christ* translated into the Shawnee language by Thomas W. Alford was published by Dr. William A. Galloway, Xenia, Ohio in 1929. One edition of 500 copies was a gift to the Shawnees from the publisher and translator.

MORE EXPERIENCE

XXVI

A SAD thing happened near the Big Jim crossing on Little River some time during the year of 1896. William Cherokee, a nephew of my friend John King was shot and killed by Robert Sloat at a dance. Both were Shawnee Indians. Robert was arrested at once and placed in the jail at Norman, where he remained until the following year when he was tried in the district court, before Judge Keaton.

I had just finished my work with Mr. Oglesby when the trial came up and I was summoned by the prosecution to act as interpreter. Joseph Blanchard was to be interpreter for the defense. Relatives on both sides of the case were prominent Shawnees, and many witnesses were present, also many relatives and friends, all keenly interested in the trial. That was one of the first cases to be tried before a jury, when both sides were Indians. It was a very serious case and would have been a difficult one to handle, even under the old tribal law, because Robert Sloat stoutly denied the crime. Both interpreters were accepted by the court and we sat together so that we might correct each other in case of mistake in rendering the evidence. Interest was intense.

After the preliminaries were gone through the case was opened by the prosecution. Witnesses were put on the stand and sworn to tell the truth. I did the interpreting, Joe sitting listening intently.

When our side of the case was finished and the defendant's side was to be presented Joe announced that I had
better keep on interpreting. I asked to be excused, for I
was tired from so much close application and the strain
of fear that I should not make each sentence quite clear.
But after the attorneys had consulted together and with
Joe, they asked me to go on, and I did. The case proceeded;
witness after witness took the stand and testified. They
tried to prove that Robert Sloat was of good character, that
he was innocent of the crime. The attorneys hurled questions at them, and I labored to clearly interpret, but it was
evident all the time that Robert would lose the case.
Finally the defendant was placed upon the stand and the
judge asked poor Robert Sloat whom he would prefer to
interpret for him and to our surprise he named me.

I value this because it shows conclusively that I had the
confidence of the Indians and the respect of the court. It
makes a sharp contrast to a time a few years later when men
who had it in their hearts to cheat the Oklahoma Indians
of their lands refused to accept me as an interpreter.

Robert Sloat, poor fellow, had a long story to tell of his
wanderings, trying to prove an alibi, but his story was not
convincing, and he failed to make the jury believe him. He
was sentenced to serve a long term in the penitentiary.
However, he was pardoned after a few years and came
home afflicted with some incurable disease and died soon
after regaining his freedom.

About this time—1896-97—the Shawnee Boarding School
had reached the highest efficiency of any time during its
existence as an educational institution, under the able
management and constant care of the superintendent,
Mrs. Mary C. Williams, whose ability as a teacher was
augmented by a deep personal interest and sympathy for
her pupils. She has gathered about her able assistants who

[169]

worked for the best interests of the children entrusted to their care. Superintendent and teachers were carrying out the purposes of the government simply and fully. Among the most prominent of her assistants was Miss Edith Reid, now Mrs. Louis C. Tyner, of Ponca City, who was untiring in her efforts for the advancement of her pupils and in their personal welfare. Since leaving the Indian service Mrs. Tyner has made for herself a recognized place in the social life of the state and has retained the love of the people with whom she worked. Other teachers labored just as diligently and are remembered just as lovingly by their former pupils. The Friends' Mission too, seemed to be doing a glorious work. There was life, activity, and a strong social influence at the mission and at the school; it seemed that young people who went there to school and attended the services were in a fair way to learn the better side of civilization. They were taking this influence into their homes too, and a general quickening of interest was evident among the people.

But at the end of the school term of 1897, through the contrivance of a special agent whose only desire it seemed was to keep in view the buttered side of his bread, Mrs. Williams was transferred to the Sauk and Fox school. It came as a rude shock to the parents of pupils in the Shawnee school and they applied to the Business Committee to try to have her returned. The Committee earnestly petitioned the Commissioner of Indian Affairs to have Mrs. Williams returned to the Shawnee school, but the petition was unheeded. Instead of coming back, Mrs. Williams was finally sent to a larger school in the far West, where she died in the harness, so to speak.

About this time, during the last years of the old century, changes were taking place rapidly in the country. The fame of the two territories, Oklahoma and Indian Territory, as farming country, as a place where business opportunities were unlimited and where investments flourished, had spread all over the nation. The country still was looked upon as a frontier, but the element of danger no longer was present, hardships were not unavoidable—and people were flocking here in vast numbers.

One railroad had been built through the country, others were talked of; little towns and larger towns were feeling the great wave of prosperity that was sweeping through the country. Is it any wonder that gangsters and politicians were in evidence, "going to and fro in the land and walking up and down in it"?

As the number of white people increased in the country, there was an increasing dissatisfaction among the Shawnee Indians. Big Jim and Sam Warrior continued to be absolutely antagonistic, not only to the allotting of their land, to every form of advancement, but to the advent of the white people. In this state of mind they easily fell under the influence of a gang of unscrupulous men who were working continually among the Indians, stirring them up against civilization and the government. Pretending to be their friends, they told the Indians the government was seeking to take away what liberties they now enjoyed, that their land would be taxed, and finally they would be forced to give up to the white man, even as their fathers had been forced to do. They told them the government was forcing the Indians to send their children to school so they would take the ways of the white man and forsake the faith of their fathers. I have no doubt that I was held up to them as an example of an Indian boy who had forsaken his own people and had adopted the ways of the white man.

These men advised the chiefs to have their people migrate to Mexico, where vast stretches of land were uncultivated, where wild game abounded, and they could live again as their fathers had lived, a wild, free, happy life. Indians, like other people, like to think and talk of "the good old times."

.   .   .   .

On April 15, 1897, I brought my second "White Bird" to my Bird's Nest. Miss Etta P. Messner, the teacher in the Kickapoo school whom I have mentioned before, kindly consented to take the place vacated by the mother of my boys. We were married and went together to Kansas City to bring the boys back, and we all began life together, in our own home.

THE DEATH OF BIG JIM

XXVII

THE men I have mentioned who were trying to stir up resentment in the minds of the Shawnee Indians succeeded in getting Big Jim to sign some kind of a contract in 1898. The exact nature of this contract I do not know, but it had something to do with the removal of the Shawnee Indians to Mexico and was the beginning of a wholesale scheme to deprive the Indians in Oklahoma of their land.

This contract was illegal, even under the old tribal law, because it was signed in secret council, in which no other member of the Shawnee tribe was present. There is no doubt that the chief thought he would be able to influence most of his tribesmen to go to Mexico, and that very alluring and false promises were made by the men who induced him to sign the contract.

Big Jim was taken to Washington, and evidently a caucus was held with some members of the United State Senate (judging from later actions of certain members of that body).

Meantime, rumors of the pressure that was being brought to bear on my uncle had been coming to me and to other members of the Business Committee. When we heard of this contract we immediately took steps to prevent the carrying out of the project. We also sent to the Commissioner of Indian Affairs a true report of conditions and circumstances that led up to the signing of the contract.

We found that a member of the Business Committee was involved in the scheme to defraud the Shawnees, and a council of the whole tribe was called to examine the member. The conclusions of this council were submitted to the Indian Agent and resulted in the dismissal of the guilty member from the Committee. This exposure temporarily thwarted the plans of the gang, but the idea had not been given up, and sinister influences were working continually, agitating the subject of migration and stirring up antagonism against the plans of the Indian Agent.

To add to the misfortune of the Shawnees at that time our chief, White Turkey, who had succeeded Joe Ellis and held some of his progressive ideas, died on November 26, 1899. His death was most grievous, especially at that critical time. With him ended the pure blood of the Tha-we-gi-la clan, for he left no descendant. My friend John King was next in line for chief, but as the government no longer recognized tribal laws, chieftainship was an empty honor and John King would not accept it. He was a member of the Business Committee and as such had some real authority.

With the strong influence of White Turkey gone the men trying to influence Big Jim to take his band to Mexico were more successful. Unable to make a wholesale robbery, they still cherished the plan of getting a number of the Indians to vacate their Oklahoma land which would thus be made available for their gang. Big Jim had a large following, but there were some of his band who realized that I knew more about the government than he did, and listened to my advice. However discontent continued to grow, and bitter feeling prevailed.

In the summer of 1900 Big Jim set out to Mexico with a small party of his chosen braves to find a place where they might take their families and make their homes. My own brother David was among the number. Arriving with his company among the friendly Mexican Kickapoos who were living in Nacemiento, west of the town of Sabinas, state of Coahula, the party found an epidemic of smallpox raging among the Indians. The chief and his whole company were exposed to the disease before they knew it.

The kind Kickapoos assured the visiting brothers that they would be properly cared for if they took the disease, but they decided to return to Oklahoma at once. My brother David left secretly that same night on horseback. He rode as hard as he could and reached home just in time to take the disease, from which he died after a short illness, on September 29, 1900. The rest of the party left for home the next morning, notwithstanding the advice and kind offers of the Kickapoos. Retracing their steps homeward they were discovered at Sabinas, and placed under quarantine on the bank of the river below the town.

There my Uncle Big Jim took the dreadful disease, to which he succumbed September 30, 1900, and was buried on the bank of the river, without ceremony. Thus ended the career of a chief, who except for his fight against civilization was a noble character. He was devoted to his people, standing strong for honesty and upright conduct, loyal and true to the traditions of his people. Only two of the entire company escaped the disease alive, and after a time returned to their homes in Oklahoma, to tell the pitiful tale of the death of the others and their simple burial of their chief. Think of a chief being buried without ceremony!

Sad as was this circumstance, it ended the work of "the gang" among the Shawnees. Possibly Big Jim saw his mistake during those last miserable days and counseled those who were left to warn the people at home. Who can say what were his emotions during his last lonely hours, when he waited for the disease to appear, and those before he died in a strange land, untended by any loving hand?

The Business Committee and the more progressive leaders were able to reason with the people to a greater degree after the influence of Big Jim was removed and they did not resent the advancing civilization so desperately any more. After the death of Big Jim the Shawnees were hesitating, puzzled about what they should do—whom they should make their principal chief on account of the potency of the Mee-saw-mi which is the life of the clan and requires that the principal chief should be of pure Tha-we-gi-la blood.

Big Jim was succeeded by his son Little Jim (To-tom-mo), who still is chief of the Shawnees. He is like his father in many ways, but has an educated, intelligent wife. She went to school at the Shawnee Boarding School and is a woman of considerable accomplishment. Let us hope that their children will inherit the sterling qualities of their grandfather and combine them with the gentler intelligence of their mother and thereby become characters worthy of their honorable ancestors.

At this time my dear friend John King died at his home, near Sunny Side farm, between Dale and McLoud. He had retired from the mercantile business to his farm, where he was living happily with his wife and one child, a daughter about one year old.

THE DAWN OF A NEW CENTURY

XXVIII

THE most important thing that happened to the Shawnee Indians in the year 1900, other than the death of Big Jim, and breaking down the influence of "the gang," was the establishment of their agency at their school. Although the school had been controlled by the government for several years it still was known to the people of the community, and among the Indians themselves as the Mission School, or the Friends' Mission. In that year the management of the Shawnee and Pottawatomie tribes was moved from the Sauk and Fox Agency and a new agency was organized at the location where it now stands, adjoining the school campus, about one mile from the city of Shawnee. At the same time Frank A. Thackery was appointed disbursing agent and superintendent of the Shawnee school, thus combining the work of the agent with that of school superintendent. Another important change was the placing of all employees of the Indian service on a Civil Service basis, doing away with the old "political spoils" system, which always was detrimental to good management.

There were many other changes of lesser importance. In fact, as I look back on those first few years of the new century they seem like a blur in my memory, so rapidly were changes taking place, and a new order of things being substituted. I have wondered if it was thus in other parts of the country, or if the condition was peculiar to the development of a new territory into a state. It was as if Father

[177]

Time had decided that the beginning of a new century was the logical time to change the old order of things. Constructive forces had long been at work, and at that particular time they seemed to culminate in revealing evidence.

As for myself, I was only a spectator at that time, scarcely noting the changes as they occurred, and certainly not then concerned with their significance. My second wife, who always had been a frail little body, developed tuberculosis soon after our marriage. She had little strength to fight such a disease. I had to stay at home most of the time and give my attention to domestic affairs instead of public duties. In the spring of 1901 I had a severe case of smallpox. After my recovery I took my wife to Colorado believing the change might restore her health, and my own be benefited.

The Colorado climate did seem to help my wife for a time, and I stayed on there with her until fall, when business affairs forced me to return home. I insisted that she remain, but she refused to consider staying without me, so we returned together.

After I had arranged my personal affairs the Business Committee elected three members to go to Washington to press some lost property claim that had been pending for twenty years. Naturally I was chosen as chairman of the delegation.

Learning that Aunty Kirk, who still was a missionary among the Indians, was going to Washington about that time, my wife decided that she would accompany me, and we all made the trip together, which added greatly to its pleasure. Arriving in Washington we were invited to stay in the home of Colonel Robert Kirk, a relative of Aunty Kirk. The whole family treated us in a very hospitable manner, and Colonel Kirk assisted the Committee in getting its business attended to although the claim was not allowed at that time. We spent two weeks in Washington and had a very pleasant visit at my Alma Mater, Hampton Institute. When we started home we stopped at Xenia, Ohio where Aunty Kirk visited her daughter, and we spent two very happy days visiting places of historic interest. Near there was the old Cha-lah-kaw-tha town of the Shawnees where my great-grandfather (the noted Tecumseh) was born, about the year 1768. We left Aunty Kirk for a more extended visit with her daughter and came on home.

My wife's health continued to fail until May 4, 1902 when she passed away and was buried in the mission cemetery. Again I was left alone with my boys. I put the boys in the Shawnee school and gave most of my time to the work of the Business Committee.

My work for the Business Committee took me into the office of Agent Frank Thackery a good deal. From my first dealings with the man I knew that the Indians had a true friend in him. In the years that followed this fact was proven many times, as also was established the fact that they needed a friend.

The mighty forces that had combined to make of this country a land of opportunity, brought together so many different elements of humanity, so many unscrupulous villains who were determined to get possession of land that belonged to the Indians, that it took a man with strength of character and courage to protect these "children of nature." That Frank Thackery possessed strength and infinite patience and courage, was proven to me many times. It was evidenced once when we made a trip together into southern Texas to find a Shawnee Indian woman who had married a Mexican. It was Thackery's business to find her as an agent of the government; it was my duty as a member of the Business Committee. Her case was a test case and came about in the following manner. Someone who was constantly checking up on the Indians to see if they were living

[179]

on their allotted land—ready to file a claim himself if the real owners were away—found the woman was absent from her claim, and was ready to file a homestead claim on her allotment. Much land was illegally secured in this way by unscrupulous persons. But this case was reported to Thackery and he set out to ascertain the truth in the matter, to find the woman and her children who were entitled to protection.

It was reported that the woman's husband had taken her to Mexico, and we followed all clues that were suggested to us. We first traced the woman to Mexico, then back into Texas. The trip was an unusually hard one. We rode many days over a rough country, under a blistering sun, with scarcely enough water or food. Finally we found an old Mexican woman who told us the young Indian woman was dead. Thackery must have positive proof, so this took many more days of tiresome travel and much weary waiting and patient searching before we did get proof that the woman and both her children had died of smallpox at San Angelo, Texas. He also verified the fact that the children had been christened before they died.

After this trip, Thackery and I had a pretty good understanding of each other, for we spent a great many hours alone together on that trip, and I think I read deep into the man's mind and heart.

LIFE AT BIRD'S NEST

XXIX

IN 1903 I again entered the U. S. Indian Service when I received an appointment as special clerk to prepare a family register of the Absentee Shawnee tribe. I had started such a register for my own convenience and for the use of the Business Committee, and the facts that I had already acquired were useful in compiling the work for the government, which soon was finished. I then took a Civil Service examination and in due time received an appointment and was assigned as chief clerk in the agency under Thackery.

In May of the same year I took the widow of my beloved friend John King for my own wife, my third "Bird," thus fulfilling the promise we had made to each other when we were boys together at Hampton. He had married a lovely Shawnee girl who had been educated at the Shawnee Boarding School. His little daughter Etta I reared to womanhood as my own. She was a beautiful girl and had many of the noble characteristics for which I had loved her father. She developed into a woman any man might be proud to call daughter; she was distinctly a credit to her race. Etta graduated from the Shawnee highschool and then from the University of Kansas, after which she taught a year in the Pawnee Indian School. She then was married to George A. Stacy, a young engineer from Virginia. They lived very happily for several years in the state of Arizona. They came to make us a visit in 1926, and unfortunately

Etta died here in our home, leaving two little girls, an infant of a few days and an older child of three years. We took the infant to rear as our own, but Etta's husband took the older child to his mother in Virginia.

Soon after I had taken my third "Bird" my eldest son Pierre went east to school, and if anyone thinks that Indians are lacking in affection or are unemotional let him read the following letter which was written in response to one I had written to my second son Reece, in which I had said that it seemed that our Pierre had forgotten the Bird's Nest, and the old father bird.

Washington, D. C.
April 19, 1904

To the Bird's Nest,
My dear Father:

Reece sent me your letter and I was very glad to get it. You must never think that I will ever forget the Bird's Nest, or the "Old Birds." I think I can remember a great deal about the Bird's Nest. At first a long time ago, I can remember the view, east and south of the old unpainted comfortable abode we called home, and to my mind it was the best home I ever knew. To the east from the house stretched the rolling grassland with a few scattering trees lining the tops of the hills in the distance.

As one glanced towards the north, his sight came in contact with the dense timber and thickets which lined the banks of Squirrel and Wildcat creeks as they neared the river. To the northwest the dense woods drew nearer the house and three tall cottonwoods stood silent sentinels that guarded the old stage line road, as it crossed Wildcat Creek at this point.

Between the woods and the house was an orchard of young peach trees and young apple trees, the latter had very ragged and rough bark where cottontails had gnawed them.

To the south the rolling grassland faded away until it reached the brow of the hill, where it seemed to end in a forest of scrub oaks and sumac. As I remember it, in those early days there was only one house in sight, that of "Sigers'" to the southwest.

The house "Bird's Nest" was surrounded by a picket fence that one might say was "home-made." Just back of it stood the old well with its old oaken bucket. Southwest of the house was a log cabin that was used for the dining-room and kitchen. The yard had several oak trees, some mulberry trees, and a large walnut tree, also some shrubbery. I must not forget to mention that in a certain corner of the yard was a nest of sand burs, which were the terror of two small boys that ranged the yard bare-legged in summer.

Many cattle grazed on the rolling hills, and the small boys watched eagerly for some of them to come home, when they would be milked by "Papa" and the hired man.

On Sunday mornings one could hear the clear tones of the Mission church bell calling, calling. Then two little boys, with Papa and Mama and baby Paul would lock the door and go through the back yard gate out to the old stage road that led across the creek, through the pasture and by the old public well to the Mission church.

Here they would go in and take their seats. The people were coming in quietly, one by one, two by two. First old Mrs. Bourbonais would come leading her husband who came on crutches. Then others came whose faces are remembered, but whose names are forgotten.

Then came in several ladies followed by a great many Indian girls, who wore all the same kind of hats, with two tails of ribbon hanging down their backs. These were followed by Indian boys in uniform of the school, who drew pictures in the hymn books and made faces at the tall straight old gentleman (when he wasn't looking) with the flowing white beard, who was trying to tell them of Jesus, who came into the world to save them.

Now we will go back to the boys, Reese and me. The smaller one teased restlessly and could not "sit still close to Mama" as he was admonished to do. Presently he would trot over to a little woman who was holding out her hand to him. He would climb into her lap and call her "Aunty Kirk." The older boy would have followed, but he was checked by his father, who said that Aunty Kirk could not take care of us all. So he sat between Papa and Mama, and looked about for something to do, then played with the baby's toes, until the baby resenting such treatment voiced his resentment. When Mama looked down she would see only a boy sitting still, trying hard not to appear guilty. Presently the father would take the boy into his arms, and soon he would be fast asleep.

After the service was over the family would tarry a few minutes to speak with friends, then go home to a dinner of chicken, or quail, or perhaps wild turkey. After the dinner the children would take a nap on a buffalo robe, maybe a wagon sheet, spread in the shade of the walnut tree, if the day was warm.

Several years after this a great many people came into the country. Towns sprang up where before cottontails were holding undisputed domain. Zack and Bailey came, the house was moved, the cabin torn down, a cellar dug, and a large new log house was built over it.

But after all was done that could be done for the comfort of the family, the hand of God came and claimed

His own. But the Great Spirit of my father and the God of my mother did not forsake the family.

The three boys went to the Kickapoo Mission and took turns living with a kind lady in Kansas City and going to school there. But while we were living at the Mission what was it that we lived for? We learned our lessons, played games, learned to shoot with our bows and arrows, and did everything we could to pass the time away until Saturday night would come, when we knew that our Papa would come to us. Then those week days that you could spend with us, when we took long walks, hunting or just alone together in the woods.

By and by we had a teacher named Etta. She came and lived with us at Bird's Nest, and after that those first days that I have mentioned were lived over again, to a certain extent.

But the boys were older and would work some. The oldest was "Papa's boy." I do not mean that he did not love his stepmother, but that he and his father were companions.

After several years of this life the home again was broken up. The Angel of Death again visited the household. The older boy went away to school, the little boys were put into boarding school, and the poor old father bird was left alone in the nest.

What could the old bird do? Why, what all lonesome old birds do when left alone—get another mate!

This was received with great cheer and thankfulness on the part of the birds. The older young bird is very glad that he has a little sister, Etta King, as well as a kind stepmother.

Father, do you think I ever could forget my home or my people and kinsmen?

I have written this, just what came into my mind, as I hastily reviewed the past. I wanted to see if I was forgetting my home—and I think that I am not forgetting much.

Pierre

AN ATTEMPTED LAND SWINDLE

XXX

WHEN I went into the Indian service as chief clerk of the Shawnee Agency under Frank Thackery I found that the propaganda that had been sown among the Shawnees, causing so much sorrow and confusion, was being dealt out to the Kickapoos and other tribes under that agency. The Kickapoos like the Shawnees were in a very unsettled condition, many of them holding just such views about education and civilization in general as Big Jim and his band of followers had held.

Some of the Kickapoos had refused to accept their allotments and had no visible means of livelihood. Poverty, even actual hunger, abounded, where a little industry might have produced plenty, for the Kickapoo country was very rich and fertile land. Thus it offered even a greater temptation to those who hoped to profit by the Indians' dissatisfaction. In their unhappy state they were especially at the mercy of the unscrupulous gang who worked ceaselessly among them.

Some member of the Kickapoo tribe came to the office almost daily with a complaint. One would say he "had been informed" that the government was going to take his children away from him and send them to school, and "make white people out of them." Some would complain that they had been told that they would have to pay heavy taxes on their land, and if they failed to pay they would be sent to jail. (The civilized mind can hardly conceive the horror

[187]

that the word "jail" means to an Indian.) Others had been told that there soon would be a war, when all the Kicka- poos would be killed and their land given to the white people. The poor creatures were in a desperate state of un- happiness.

It was evident that all this "information" was being furnished by the very same men who had tried to induce the Shawnees to migrate to Mexico, and had persuaded Big Jim to sign the contract before mentioned, a scheme that only his untimely death had prevented his carrying out. Although the work of the Business Committee had held it back for a while, I feel sure we would have been defeated in the end, and a large number of the Shawnee Indians would have been paupers in Mexico if the old chief had lived. This scheme was sponsored by powerful men whose influence reached to officials of the national government. In fact there were men involved in the scheme who are so prominent in the country today that were I to mention their names a national scandal would be raised. This I have no intention of doing, but I do intend to file a true account of the affair with the Oklahoma Historical Society because it rightly belongs in the history of the Oklahoma Indians.

I fought this gang single-handed, as an individual Indian, as a member of the Business Committee of my tribe, and then as a representative of the Indian service after I went into Thackery's office, altogether for more than ten years, and I feel that some mention of my experience should be given in this record of my life work, hence I shall give a brief account of it here.

In the beginning it was the big idea of the gang to work on the Indians' aversion to civilization until they volun- tarily abandoned their allotments and left the country. As there no longer was any place in the United States where they might have free possession of land, they were induced to go to Mexico. It did not matter to these men that Shawnee Indians had no claim on Mexican land or citizenship, or that they had no idea of business or ability to earn their daily bread by toil in the market places. *To get possession of their land was the only thought of those in the game.*

But the laws of the country forbade the Indians to sell their land. Some kind-hearted lawmakers had taken that means of safeguarding the interest of the government's wards. But there was a way to get around that law, provided members of Congress could be induced to concur in the game.

This was not such a hard thing to do as it seemed to be. The Indians were induced to leave the country, go for an extended visit with their friends in Mexico, until Congress could pass a law, declaring them nonresidents of the United States and giving them the privilege of selling their land here. This was accomplished.

A number of Kickapoo Indians were kept in Mexico, entertained, fed, given plenty of whisky to drink, guarded like cattle, until that law was passed by Congress and the bill signed by the president of the United States. Then the Indians sold their land in Oklahoma for sums far below its actual value. They lost their citizenship in the United States and gained none in Mexico.

The heroic work of Frank Thackery, who followed the Indians to Mexico and kept untiringly on the job, resulted in the injustice being brought to the Commissioner of Indian Affairs and the Department of Justice in its true light, and action was taken to annul the sales.

The case dragged through the courts for several months. It was a great legal fight, and the whole country was interested in it. Some of the tools of the real perpetrators of the crime were thrown into prison, but were finally re-leased after citizenship was restored to the Kickapoos, and their land was voluntarily returned to them.

Did I have a part in defeating this gang? Thackery says that I did; I know that I did. Yet when "the investigating committee" sent by the United States Senate Committee on Indian Affairs was taking testimony in the case, it refused to accept me as an interpreter, and took an un-educated Kickapoo boy whose vocabulary consisted of less than three hundred words as their interpreter. However, in the final adjustment when the Mexican government demanded an investigation, both this government and the government of Mexico accepted me as interpreter.[1]

I think that the work of Frank Thackery, George Outcelt, John Embry, and a few others who took part in this affair deserves the everlasting gratitude of the people for prevent-ing such a disgrace to the nation as that transaction would have been. That I, too, had a small part in the work, is one of the proudest achievements of my life.

1. The Mexican government resented the intrusion of the Indians who were citizens of Oklahoma and demanded the arrest of those who perpetrated the injus-tice. It is very likely there might have been international trouble, but a revolution broke out in Mexico about that time, the government was changed and the matter dropped. Hence, charges were dropped against United States citizens who then were in jail.

OKLAHOMA BECOMES A STATE

XXXI

DURING those strenuous months and years when Indian history was adding another chapter to its tragic story, and the Indians themselves were floundering through a sea of doubt, indecision, and despair, distrusting their friends and accepting advice from their enemies, fighting against the inevitable—the whole country was in a state of political turmoil. The two territories, Oklahoma Territory and Indian Territory, had been recognized as being a part of the richest section of the United States. Land that had been considered worthless when it was assigned to the Indians for their permanent home had turned out to be of inestimable value, not only as an agricultural country but for its mineral resources.

Stories of the ease with which the Indians could be cheated were current wherever newspapers were read. Many of the tribes still were receiving annuity payments, those who had sold their land were being paid for it— money was supposed to flow freely through legitimate channels of trade, too. Then there were exaggerated stories of the wonderful opportunities for development of big business. All this resulted in a steady stream of immigration, making perhaps the most cosmopolitan population of any of the midwest states.

A great many people who had failed in other states came into the new territory to begin again, and it had long been a refuge for outlaws and criminals. Naturally the country was considered to be in a very immoral condition by people in the older states, especially those "back East." I remember hearing an evangelist who was holding a religious revival tell a story that illustrates the general opinion of Oklahoma Territory.

A little girl whose family was moving to Oklahoma was saying her prayers, and after the usual "Now I lay me down to sleep" and a petition for a blessing and tender care of each individual member of the family, the devout little creature added, "Now goodbye, dear Lord. We are going to move to Oklahoma tomorrow."

Another story I heard is indicative of the situation in the city of Shawnee. It was at the time that the Santa Fe railroad was trying to get a right of way through the town, and the citizens were trying to raise a bonus for the road to insure its coming at this point. One of the business men who was a staunch friend and admirer of William Jennings Bryan and believed in his well-known policy of "free coinage of silver," opposed the raising of the bonus for the railroad. In a speech he made at a gathering of the citizens he cried, "We don't need another railroad anyhow. We already have a good town, and a ratio of sixteen to one." meaning sixteen saloons to one railroad.

But the bonus was raised, and the Santa Fe railroad built through the town, which continued to grow, and the country continued to develop. In fact the country had developed so fast and there were so many people here, that a great hue and cry went up for statehood. Some politicians favored the admission of the two territories into the Union as one state, others opposed that measure and strove for separate recognition for the two.

The political party then in power having the appointment of all officers opposed the admission of either of the territories as states. There was a great deal of turmoil over the issue. It is possible that the disgrace attached to the Kickapoo Land Fraud case and the fear of further publicity by some of those opposed to the admission broke down the barriers.

Be that as it may, the two territories were admitted as one state on November 16, 1907, amid great rejoicing and celebrating by the white people. The "red man's country" soon became one of the most thoroughly organized states in the Union and the first one in which the original owners of the land, the American Indians, remained in any large number as equal citizens with the white race, or had any part in the organization or formation of the government.

When all of the Indian population of the state realize this fact and the privilege that it conveys, and add to their inborn pride of race the true pride of American citizenship, the race will become a really great factor in the commonwealth.

HERE I SHALL BE UNTIL THE END

XXXII

WHEN the Kickapoo Land Fraud case was settled I offered my resignation as chief clerk in the Shawnee Agency but retained my position as chairman of the Business Committee, which office I still hold. The duties incumbent to that office are growing less and less every year, as more of our young people are learning to understand business matters and to act for themselves.

Frank Thackery was promoted to another branch of the Indian service in 1910, and after he left the Shawnee Boarding School it gradually declined. With statehood came a better system of public schools; many of the Indian children spoke English, and it was considered best that they attend public schools with the white children in the district in which they live. The government pays tuition for the Indian children to the district which they attend, which has helped materially in the building up of the rural school system.

The Shawnee Boarding School was closed in 1919. The valuable buildings were left to fall into ruins, the grounds and walks were overrun with weeds and straggling wild flowers and vines, unhappy refuge for thousands of birds, whose songs seem to take on a sad note. Especially is this true of the doves, whose plaintive notes will haunt a visitor for days.

The closing of the school made the presence of the Friends' Mission unnecessary, and the little white church that had played such an inestimable part in the civilization of our people was abandoned. Its bell hung rusting and unused in the decaying belfry. The little manse[1] with its flagstone walks, beds of poppies, hollyhocks, tall cedars, trailing rose vines, and honeysuckle was untenanted; its only occupants were the ghostly memories of other days.

But the ways of civilization, which a large number of the Indians had imperfectly adopted, had brought disaster to their health. The Indian Department became aware that tuberculosis was taking a heavy toll among the older generation, and unless some drastic measures were adopted at once the younger one soon would be infected with the disease. After consideration it was decided to turn the old school into a sanitarium for tubercular patients. This was done, and the buildings were remodeled, repaired, and fully equipped for treatment of such cases.[2] It was opened for tubercular patients, especially children afflicted with the disease in its early stages. Many have overcome the disease, a few have been found incurable, and still are receiving care, while a few have passed on. A school is maintained in connection with the sanitarium where those who are able to study may do so. At the time the sanitarium was opened the Philadelphia Society of Friends still owned the mission property, but kept no missionary there. Charles Wooten, a minister of that faith, bought the property and a little farm adjoining, and opened the mission again at his own expense. He and his wife give freely of their time to the inmates of

1. The manse recently was destroyed by fire, and a substantial farmhouse now stands on the location, which is know as "Wayside Farm." The mission too has been abandoned since Mr. Alford's manuscript was completed.

2. A new hospital building which is one of the best in the United States, fully equipped with all modern appliances for the treatment of tuberculosis has been completed at the Shawnee sanitarium. A school and a therapy department are features of importance at the institution, which is under the management of Doctor David W. Gillick who is known nationally for his skill in the treatment of tuberculosis.

the sanitarium and keep alive the missionary spirit in the little white church which has withstood the storms of so many years. Its silver toned bell that hung silent for years may again be heard on a clear Sunday morning calling, calling all in the neighborhood to come and worship at its simple altar.

In 1912 the business of the Sauk and Fox and Iowa tribes was transferred to the Shawnee Agency. Thus five tribes are under the jurisdiction of the agency here.

Never before has the strong arm of the government so thoroughly reached out to care for and protect its Indian wards as it does at the present time. In fact an Indian agent of today is, in reality, the head of a large family with a corps of efficient specialists at his command. Doctors, lawyers, teachers, nurses, all experts in their line, are ready to attend to the needs of his family—the Indians under his care.

The government physician looks after the health of the people, and the well-being of the Indian child is carefully looked after until he reaches school age. There is a school inspector whose business it is to see that Indian children are kept in school. There still are many Indian parents who do not care to send their children to school, and it sometimes is necessary to force parents to send their children to school, even as compulsory school laws are enforced among white people. The inspector keeps a record of all Indian children under the agency for which he is responsible, their progress and development are checked with records kept by their teachers. Their habits are guarded, and they are given regular physical examinations.

Any Indian child that shows any unusual talent along any line is encouraged to develop that talent. After the child completes the grammar school he is encouraged to enter some higher school where he may take training in any subject he may care to pursue. If he desires to become a farmer there are experts to give him instruction in agricultural methods; he is trained in practical as well as scientific work.

The girls are taught practical home-making and like their brothers may take special training along any line they may prefer. Some members of our tribe have distinguished themselves by their artistic achievement.

When these young people go out into the world to take their places as citizens they still are looked after, their interests guarded, although they are absolutely free. Expert advice is theirs for the asking. If they are ill they may receive medical attention from physicians who thoroughly understand the peculiarities of their patients. In case of death an Indian's funeral is arranged for, and his estate probated.

Someone might ask, what is the result of all this care, this supervision? How much has it added to their civilization?

I think to answer this question one must ask, what is civilization? *Our young people are taking up the ways of the white people.* Whether that will lead them to a higher civilization or to a more flagrant vaunting of their freedom, I do not know.

To be sure there are social distinctions among the Indians that mark the intelligence of their families, just as there are among all other races. The more intelligent class of our young people are keeping pace with the same class among their white neighbors. They attend the same high schools, they wear the same fashions in clothing, they read the same books, attend the same theater. They exercise the same privilege accorded them by the Constitution of the United States to "pursue happiness" in just the same way that white people do. In fact a great many of our young people have acquired "culture."

The young men drive high-powered cars, drink a little, perhaps gamble a little. They have learned to woo the female of the species in just the same ardent manner that their white brothers use. Our girls of today wear a different kind of "paint" to that used by their ancestors, they wear their hair short, dress in Paris fashion, and get their finger nails manicured, just exactly like their white friends do.

But is all this civilization?

A great many of our young people are floundering about. They have lost their bearings, because they have lost the tenacious, underlying strength of their forefathers, and have not attained any of their own. They have discarded the faith of their parents and have not adopted the religion of the white man. In every human heart there is a deep spiritual hunger for an abiding, steadfast faith, a positive, satisfying belief in some future existence. Such a faith stabilizes character, and many of our young people have no such anchor for their souls.

Then some of them are confused by the conflict of a new social intercourse with the whites. They feel a sort of difference in the point of view and are not sure about the attitude they should take. Some have keen intelligence and sparkling wit and take their places in the circle to which they belong.

Contrary to the general impression the Indian race is not "dying out." At least the Shawnees are not. They are just gradually losing their identity. There now are so many intermarriages with the white people that soon there will be no "pure blood Indian" or fullbloods among our people. In that we are no different from other races, and I believe the time will come when our contribution to the sterling qualities of the American people will be recognized and appreciated.

Since leaving the Indian service I have lived quietly at my old home, the same "Bird's Nest." My own sons and daughters are among those I have mentioned as going out into the tide of life, taking their places in the economic life of the country. I have tried to instill into their hearts and minds some of the principles of my people, and I believe that I have succeeded.

Here I shall remain until the end.

A SKETCH OF HISTORY OF
ABSENTEE SHAWNEES

*This is an exact copy of the first part of the brief history of the
Absentee Shawnees by Mr. Alford*

ACCORDING to their ancient traditional history the Shawnee
Nation is divided into five clans or sects: viz: Tha-we-gi-la, Cha-lah-gaw-tha (Chillicothe), Pec-ku-we, Kis-po-go, and May-ko-jay.
The first two mentioned are the principal or national clans from either
of which comes the ruler of the nation who is called principal chief, and
is also chief of his own clan. But the rest are subordinate; each has its
own chief but his authority does not extend beyond his own clan.

Naturally the two principal clans had been in rivalry against each
other from time immemorial, dividing the subordinate clans to their
sides thus: The Pec-ku-we and Kis-po-go allied to the Tha-we-gi-la
clan composing the Absentee Shawnee tribe as it is today, while the
May-ko-jay allied to the Cha-lah-gaw-tha clan, composing the Kansas
or Cherokee Shawnees of today.

As the years of war among Indians rolled away and the entrance
of the white race into this country resulted in more wars and conten-
tions, the Tha-we-gi-la group became more or less advocates of peace,
while the other group held more or less for war for their country until
all were exterminated. Of course this is all nonsense to the government;
regardless of how it is viewed, this is the real, inside history of the
Shawnees which finally led to their division into two tribes of the
nation today.

Since the defeat of the French in 1763 and consequently the sur-
render of all their lands by the King of France to the King of England
which awakened their minds to the power of the English the chiefs of
all the clans began to hold deliberations from time to time which lasted
several years to determine their future policy of peace or war with the
English. But they evidently failed to agree. Hence after one of their
great battles in 1774 against the English at Point Pleasant where
the chief Bucksinwa, father of Tecumtha (or Tecumseh) was killed,

the actual separation of the peace advocates took place. Several other Shawnee chiefs took part in this battle; among them was chief Kikuskawlowa (or Kishkalwa) who was unwilling any longer to be embroiled with the Americans with whom he was well disposed, or to take any part in the contest which was about to be commenced between Great Britain and the colonies. He removed a great part of the Tha-we-gi-la clan to the south and there united with the rest living among the Creeks; and later returned to the shores of the Ohio River—to their "homeland" (now the state of Kentucky), for the last time; and from thence in 1785 left the United States and went into the Spanish Territory west of the Mississippi River, as their own statement attests made in a treaty council held in 1815 at St. Louis by William Clark and others representing the government. In 1793 the Spanish government granted them land twenty-five miles square at Cape Girardeau, now Cape Girardeau County, Missouri.

In the spring of 1779 the rest of the Pec-ku-we and Kis-po-go clans from their principal town called Peckuwe, or Piqua, and later known as Old Chillicothe, now Old Town, Ohio, and from elsewhere on the Miami valleys—1200 warriors, women, and children—left and joined their brethren at Cape Girardeau.

The last but a small party, those spoken of as the "hostile party," followed in a roundabout way to the south among the Creeks where they were in 1792, and from thence to Cape Girardeau.

This completes the emigration of the peace advocates then known as Missouri Shawnees, now as the Absentee Shawnees of the state of Oklahoma. They took no part in the war of 1794 nor in that of 1812 nor has this portion of the Shawnees ever been engaged against the Americans since the decisive battle of Point Pleasant. Perhaps this is the reason why record of their history is quite scanty; because they are peaceable the government always neglected or ignored their interests. They never received any annuities and have always been self-supporting as the reports of the commissioners of Indian affairs later attested. At that time the country towards Mexico was a wilderness abounding in game and fur bearing animals of all kinds which supplied them with not only subsistence but all the necessaries of life; for what they could not raise and manufacture themselves they purchased with skins and furs.

Some time after they had received the grant of land at Cape Girardeau a great portion of them went into the wilderness leaving a few families behind to occupy and take care of it, thinking to keep it as a permanent home whenever they chose to return to it. But during their sojourn those who were left behind, known later as the Black Bob band entered into a treaty November 7, 1825 with the United States and received land—50 miles square near the Kansas River west of Missouri in lieu of the land granted them at Cape Girardeau.

Happily however the sojourners in Mexico obtained another grant of land from the Mexican government on Sabine River, now part of eastern Texas. During the year 1832 Gen. Sam Houston was appointed by Mexican authorities to settle the boundary dispute with the Indians. But he soon however became imbued with the spirit of the American settlers who desired the autonomy of Texas as a state in the Republic of Mexico, and was opposed by the Mexican President Santa Anna whose arbitrary policies led to the revolt of the colonists setting up an independent state which within three years became the Republic of Texas with General Houston as its first president.

In this three years struggle he was aided by these Shawnees who were beginning to be called the Absentees by their brethren they left behind. For their aid and assistance the first legislature of the Republic of Texas made a solemn pledge to them in 1835 acknowledging their just claims to their land, setting forth the boundaries thereof; and saying further: "We solemnly declare that we will guarantee to them peaceable enjoyment of all their rights to their lands as we do our own. We solemnly declare that all grants, surveys, or locations of land within the bounds hereinafter mentioned made after the settlements of these Indians be utterly null and void."

Yet in 1839, only four years after that solemn pledge they were driven out of Texas and their lands all taken up by a company of land speculators who had obtained from the Republic a floating claim for forty leagues of land, and who, finding these Indians had the best portion of land in eastern Texas, charged them with treason, proved it by hearsay evidence, managed to have war declared against them, and when driven from the Republic these speculators floated their claims upon their lands.

They went or were driven north across the Red River into the Indian Territory, now the state of Oklahoma, and from 1840 to 1862 were residing on the frontier of the Choctaw and Creek Indian settlements. A few who had married among some western tribes went with them to the western part of Texas.

In the meantime those of the Cha-lah-gaw-tha group or war advocates remained in what is now the state of Ohio, who were hostile to the white settlements most of the time between 1755 and the treaty of Greenville in 1795. They were later assigned lands by the treaty of September 29, 1817 at Wapaghkonetta and Hog Creek on the site of the present city of Lima, Ohio; and still later by the treaty of July 20, 1831 they were given land in what now is the state of Kansas "to contain 100,000 acres within the tract of land equal to 50 miles square" previously granted to the Missouri Shawnees (now Absentee Shawnees) in lieu of their land at Cape Girardeau ceded to the United States November 7, 1825 by the few called the Black Bob band. They were at once removed—about 300 souls—from Ohio during the following year (1832-33) into this 100,000 acres assigned them—the last of the Shawnees to remove west of the Mississippi River. Again in 1854 they entered into a treaty with the United States disposing this land without any representation, knowledge, or consent of their brethren the Absentees who were then living in the Indian Territory and reserved for them a few acres of land if they should come within five years; but if they did not, the land would be sold and the proceeds reserved for them another five years—making ten years in all. But they did not notify them, how could the Absentees avail themselves of these provisions for they knew not what was being done with their land.

Soon after this treaty between the years 1861 and 1862, there was a great agitation among all the Indians in the Indian Territory caused by the Civil War which had already begun between the North and the South.

During all the times the Absentee Shawnees supported themselves without aid, received no annuity or any funds or any part thereof from the government.